FROM TYRANNY TO FREEDOM

JOHN VANDENBERGE, DDS, DD

FROM

my journey from

TYRANNY

war-torn Holland

TO

to America

FREEDOM

Tate Publishing & *Enterprises*

Published by Tate Publishing & Enterprises, LLC
127 E. Trade Center Terrace | Mustang, Oklahoma 73064 USA
1.888.361.9473 | www.tatepublishing.com

Tate Publishing is committed to excellence in the publishing industry. The company reflects the philosophy established by the founders, based on Psalm 68:11,
"The Lord gave the word and great was the company of those who published it."

Cover design by Amber Gulilat
Interior design by Stephanie Woloszyn

Published in the United States of America

ISBN: 978-1-61663-094-2
1. Biography & Autobiography / Historical
2. Biography & Autobiography / Personal Memoirs
10.07.26

DEDICATION

This book is dedicated to God, to America, and to all of those freedom fighters who have served this great land; especially those who have given their lives for our freedom, to their families, and to those serving today. It is dedicated also to my parents, who sacrificed so much; and to my parents-in-law, who received me in America with much grace and love.

WHAT THEY ARE SAYING ABOUT

FROM TYRANNY TO FREEDOM

"An incredible personal life story that is crying to be made into an inspirational movie. John has done us a great favor by sharing his and his families' awesome experiences of life. Thank God for such families."

—Richard L. Alms, PhD.

Having lived as a young man during the period of time described in *From Tyranny to Freedom,* and served in the Army Air Corps during World War II, it is impossible to sum up in a sentence or two the emotions it generates. This is a book for our time. Walk personally in the shoes of the author as he describes that terrible time experienced by real people under the cruel, godless, and dictatorial umbrella of Nazism, and then the unique comparison upon stepping into the sunshine of freedom in the United States where God was freely recognized and worshiped. This is not just another autobiography, but a personal view of historic reality. It is an admonishment to this nation, which has now legally excluded God and His moral standards in violation of our founding documents, that we are duplicating the path of Germany in the 1930s, and headed into godless socialism.

—Attorney Bernard P. Reese Jr., LLD
Trustee United States Supreme Court Historical Society

I believe the generation today must never forget the horrors of World War II. We enjoy the blessings of today because of previous generations' faith in God and their willingness to sacrifice their lives for God, for freedom, and for the better future for their children. The comparisons Dr. Vandenberge has made between the rise of Nazism and what is going on in America today are vital. If this nation does not heed messages like his we could find ourselves in a position very similar to that of Western Europe during World War II.

—The Rt. Rev. Philip C. Zampino,
Anglican Bishop, Retired

ACKNOWLEDGMENTS

Thank you to Anthony Anderson, who delivered a very moving and educational lecture at the University of Southern California on October 17, 1995. This manuscript references several photos he used in his presentation and includes some of the important information he conveyed. A special thanks to Mr. Harco Gijsbers of Beeldbank WO2 (Image Bank WW2) for giving the official permission to use the World War II photos of the Rotterdam Bombardment by the Nazis in May 1940.

Thank you to Navy History and Heritage Command for their incredible photos.

Thank you to the *Baltimore Sun* and to *The Index Journal of Greenwood, South Carolina* for their wonderful reporting.

Thank you to Roxanne Christ and Bonnie C. Harvey, Ph.D., for early editing, and to Trisha E. Calvarese, whose fine-tuned editing was great.

A special thank you to Marian Lawrence, Jeanne and John McKean and Edith Land for their unwavering support, prayers and encouragement.

lot of traffic, particularly barges transporting goods from Europe for transfer to ocean-going vessels.

Bergweg Apartment above "Assurantien"

For years, Rotterdam was second to New York City in traffic volume.

Moe and I stayed home, as usual, with Joop (Jack), my nine-month-old baby brother. I was almost four then, and I had no idea what was really happening, except that I could *feel* my mother was frightened, and so was I.

I have no memory of anything before that day—May 10, 1940. But the picture of neighbors across the street in their pajamas has been etched in my mind as the beginning of the war for me.

Jan (John), three years, eleven months old (three days before the war)

The next three days were filled with rumors, but we still had not seen any Nazi soldiers. Everybody was very nervous. On the fourth day, May 14, the situation was hopeless. The Nazis had envisioned conquering Holland in one day, but now it had taken four days, so they made it known to General Winkelman, who was in charge of the Dutch military, that if the Dutch would not surrender, all the cities in Holland would be systematically bombed. General Winkelman set up negotiations with the Nazis, but these negotiations did not go well, and the bombing began.

Rotterdam CIty Jail, City Hall, and Post Office *before* the bombing

Rotterdam City Jail, City Hall, and Post Office
after the bombing (see small arrows)

Rotterdam around the railroad station *before* bombing

Rotterdam around the railroad station *after* bombing

Pa had gone to work again in the morning on the streetcar. Soon after lunch, all hell broke loose downtown, including at his Dutch government employment office at the Kipstraat (Chicken Street). Nazi warplanes dotted the city skyline and began dropping bombs. The Dutch marines had successfully stopped the enemies at the Maas River Bridge, which is why the bombs started falling. The German war machine was very well prepared. There had been reports prior to the war that German spies had taken photographs of airfields, government buildings, and military installations as well as harbors. The Dutch government had been warned but had not taken these reports seriously.

Holland and Switzerland were two countries which had remained neutral in the First World War. Holland wanted to do that again and had not built up their military strength to meet an eventual challenge such as this one. The Royal Dutch Air Force had only five airplanes. The bombardment started to beat the Dutch military into submission.

They bombed downtown Rotterdam, flattening many buildings, stores, and inner city residences, but somehow they did not touch the city jail, city hall or the post office. At City Hall, of course, there were many important population records. The city jail would be needed to house resistant Dutchmen, and the post office was needed for mail sorting and scrutinizing business and other papers.

Some 78,000 citizens were made homeless, and over 30,000 were killed. Two thousand one hundred Dutch soldiers died, and 2,700 were wounded. During the bombardment, many children died while in school.

The bombardment "before" and "after" photos of Rotterdam have been provided at the courtesy of Anthony Anderson at the University of Southern California, which he presented at a lecture at the University on October 17, 1995.

For two weeks, quite a few Nazi soldiers were hidden before the attack in large, closed barges, which had been floated down the Rhine and Maas Rivers and were parked right in the middle of Rotterdam in the harbor, supposedly freight barges ready to be unloaded. At the right time, the doors opened, and the soldiers came out of those barges and occupied the center of Rotterdam.

Suddenly, airplanes were overhead, bombs started falling, and Pa quickly realized he had to get out of there. He ran out of his building and across the street, into the lobby of another building. He hid there for a short time and then dashed into another building, zigzagging his way toward home; and as he did, buildings behind him collapsed. The dust from pulverized structures was overwhelming, and as Pa continued to run home, he was covered with dust.

It was a good thing my father had been a long-distance runner when he was young. Once, he had won a race from Rotterdam to Gouda and back—about thirty-six miles both ways. When he came upstairs after running all the way from downtown, he was quite exhausted. His dark suit was totally white from the dust, and no doubt his lungs were filled with the stuff as well. He gasped for air and said with great effort, "We must flee. Now!" So Moe grabbed the stroller, some diapers, a little food for the baby, a few other things, and off we went. We did not know where we were going except away from downtown.

My father thought all of Rotterdam was going to be bombed. We walked as fast as we could away from bombs, explosions, and warplanes flying overhead toward Terbregge, a suburb, which Pa thought would be a little safer. As we went farther out, my father remembered that one of his colleagues, Mr. Dirkzwager, lived in the area. Pa knocked on his door and asked if we could spend the night. The man welcomed us, and we slept there that evening. Incidentally, the Kipstraat office was also destroyed during the Rotterdam bombardment, and the government employment office was relocated later to Middellandstraat. I remember visiting my father's office at that location a few times after the war.

The next day, we saw Nazi soldiers for the first time. They mostly rode around on motorcycles. At one point, one soldier stopped right in front of the house where we were staying. He took out a map to figure out where he was. Since Pa spoke German, he gingerly but courageously walked out to the man on the motorcycle and tried to strike up a conversation. Pa took that opportunity to have a look at the map he was holding and was amazed at how accurate and detailed the map was. The thing is, Pa had been trying for years to get a good map of Rotterdam but could never find one. The German spies had done an excellent job.

A couple of days later, after things had calmed down, Pa thought it was safe to return and to see if our apartment was still there. Radio announcements actually made it clear that people were encouraged to go back to their homes, or the Nazis (or others) could seize them. We had no way of knowing at this point whether we still had a place to live. As we approached our neighborhood, we were pleasantly surprised. Our apartment was still there. What a relief! Martin was so happy to find that his canary was still alive and appeared okay.

One of the things the Nazis did early was arrest some very prominent people, like bank presidents and owners and presidents of large companies, such as the Ruys Company, a big steamship company. Mr. Willem Ruys and other prominent figures were rounded up, lined up in front of a wall in the center of the city, and were promptly executed by a firing squad. The enemy put fear in the Dutch citizens so as to prevent massive uprisings or other rebellious activities.

On one occasion, some Dutch Underground men (one of whom was my cousin), had overpowered a Nazi truck. They "took care" of the driver and the other soldier, put on their uniforms, drove the truck into the Rotterdam city jail, forced their way into the prison, and unlocked the cells of some of their Underground friends and set them free. They all escaped safely.

Around 1979, I was hosting a small cable TV talk show in Howard County, Maryland, where I interviewed various people on a program called, *The Choice*. One of the people I interviewed was Dr. Ernest Cassutto, who was there with his wife. During the taping, I mentioned to him that I had read his book, *The Last Jew of Rotterdam*. He and his family had survived the war in Holland as Jews. Then, when I mentioned that one of my cousins, Arend Segaar, and others, overpowered a Nazi truck, put on German uniforms, and drove into the jail to release their friends, Dr. Cassutto almost jumped from excitement and said, "I know. I was in one of those cells!" What a moment that was. I could hardly believe it. Here I had emigrated from Holland to America in 1958, had lived in this country for about twenty years, and only then ran into this stranger who was in one of those cells in my hometown of Rotterdam in 1940.

The Dutch Underground could not continue such clandestine activities. Whenever any German soldiers were killed, the Nazis would just round up the same number of VIPs and execute them by firing squad. By the way, I always try to distinguish carefully between Nazis and the German people. The Germans are wonderful, normal people. It's Hitler's Nazis we had big problems with.

Hitler wanted to annex Holland and place it under a civilian administration with a fanatical Austrian Nazi at the head. His name was Arthur Seyss-Inquart. Hitler wanted to use the so-called "superior" racial composition of the Dutch people, certifiably one-hundred percent Aryan, to interbreed with the Germans and improve the racial purity of the new German super nation.[1] Seyss-Inquart assumed all the civilian functions and powers that formerly belonged to the Dutch crown and the government. The Austrian was a most loyal servant of Hitler and the Nazi cause.

During the first two years, he issued a vast number of decrees, but they trickled off as the occupation drew toward an end. He basically implemented policies dictated from Berlin, including economic exploitation of the Netherlands, the labor draft, and the persecution of Jews. When, at the end of the war, Hitler prepared his last will and testament, he proposed that Seyss-Inquart become the new foreign minister.

One group of Dutchmen was actually happy with the German invasion. They were members of the NSB, the Dutch Nazi Party or National-Socialistische Beweging der Nederland. The head of this group was Anton Mussert, a one-time civil engineer from Utrecht. They were more like Mussolini's fascist party initially and not so much like Hitler's.

They were also not particularly anti-Semitic, and even some Dutch Jews became NSB members. But gradually, the NSB did become more Nazi-like. Another Dutch Nazi was Rust van Tonnigen, who really wanted Holland to become part of Nazi Germany.

CHAPTER 2
SURVIVAL

The food supplies gradually dwindled throughout the five years of the war. At first, during the first year, food-rationing tickets appeared. At that time, the amount of rationed food was not too bad, but it steadily became worse and worse. I remember that the quality of milk went from milk to what seems like just white water. During the first two years or so, there was some milk, and we were able to buy some from "Aurora," the local milk store. As we had no refrigerator, Moe had to make daily trips to local shops to buy vegetables, meat, bread and other groceries as they were available.

The lady who ran the milk store was Mrs. Tollenaar. She had two sons and a daughter, Neeltje, who was mentally retarded. From time to time, Neeltje waited on my mother when she exchanged the rationing tickets for milk. In 1943–44, the Tollenaar's son, Leen, was looking for a job. He asked if Pa could help him, and Pa did find him employment with a company called Couzy, where Leen subsequently worked for many years.

The winters in Europe used to be very cold. In 1929, the Maas River actually froze over so that one could walk across the river and even ride a motorbike on the ice, as shown in the photo of my uncle Henk (Moe's brother) and aunt Nel. This would be like the Hudson River, in New York, freezing over.

Uncle Henk and Aunt Nel "on ice," Maas River, 1929

By 1944, people had become desperate for food. I remember seeing a man on the sidewalk not far from our apartment, bent down, having taken a spoon from his back pocket, to eat someone else's vomit right from the sidewalk. I know this is not very pleasant, but it was real. Combined with the scarcity of food, any food that was available was often contaminated, and many people were sick with digestive problems. Of course, medical help was scarce as well. So when my father found out that my uncle Wout's sister, Marie, was going out of town to Putte to try to get some food, he inquired if Martin, who was fifteen then, could go with her.

He stayed with the family overnight, got some food to eat, and went on to Garderen by himself, where Uncle Piet, my father's brother, lived on a small farm. Martin rode an old bicycle originally fitted with rubber tires. Bicycle tires had not been available since early in the war, and he had put a thick rope around the rims of the wheels to serve as a makeshift cushion, which worked just enough to use the bike.

On the way to Garderen, some sixty-five kilometers (40.6 miles) away, Martin was almost arrested and could have been killed when a Nazi soldier jumped out of nowhere, brandishing a rifle and pointing it at him. He was questioned as to why he was there. He did not know that a few days earlier, four Nazis had been hanged; therefore, everyone was a suspect. Fortunately, the soldier let him go.

Uncle Piet and Aunt Adrie were, of course, surprised to see Martin, who told them how bad things were in Rotterdam. There were no farms in Rotterdam, and the food shortage had reduced the city to famine conditions. Finally, Martin asked if he could get something to eat. He did not remember how stingy our uncle and aunt were. Uncle Piet said he had to ask Aunt Adrie. (Uncle Piet had to ask Aunt Adrie for everything.) After hearing their whispers in the background, Martin was given a slice of bread and a small glass of milk. By this time, he could have eaten a loaf of bread and drank a gallon of milk. Well, at least he got a good night's sleep; and he was given some potatoes, vegetables, wheat, and some other little things in the morning, for which he was very grateful. My father had given Martin one hundred guilders to buy any food he could. Pa had told him, "The money is not good for anything else anyway."

On the way back to Rotterdam, Martin found a Red Cross station in Nykerk, where he found a good night's rest and some food. It was in that town that his bike got stuck in a streetcar rail track. The front wheel of his bike was bent badly, so he could no longer use it. He started walking.

On occasion, walkers could hitch a ride with Nazi cars or trucks. The Nazis would let people ride on the fenders sometimes to prevent them from being shot on sight by the Allies. If low-flying airplanes saw people on the cars, they might have had second thoughts about bombing the cars.

My brother asked the driver of one car, a French Citroen which had large front fenders, if he could ride on one of the side fenders, but he was told " no". There were four Nazi officers in the car, and they already had two other people sitting on the fenders, so that did not work. Martin was disappointed, of course, but he walked on. A few hours later, he noticed a car burning on the road ahead. As he approached the car, he noticed that it was the same Citroen, bombed from the air, and all officers and passengers were dead. What a shock for Martin! He realized someone from above was looking out for him.

Farther down the road was the town of Jutfaas, which was about forty kilometers (25 miles) from Rotterdam, where Martin found another oasis. He ate some cream, the top layer of fresh milk, which was wonderful, along with some bacon and bread. This respite restored him for the rest of his journey home.

As he got closer to Rotterdam, he realized there was a seven o'clock curfew in the evening. He had left Jutfaas and had another forty kilometers (25 miles) to go. He heard the church bells chime announcing seven o'clock. Suddenly, out of nowhere, a horse and buggy appeared with a nice man who asked Martin where he was going. He gave Martin a ride, and Martin was grateful. He said the sound of the horse's feet were like music to his ears. As they got closer to Rotterdam, the driver told Martin they had to part. Thus, Martin had to walk (again) the rest of the way home, but at least he was closer.

Now it was a matter of dodging the Nazis to get home. He went street by street, carefully looking around each corner for any lurking enemies. When he finally came close to the Bergweg, he successfully navigated the Benthuiserstraat, and around the corner, he had to get past the *Ford* garage with open front doors, where the Nazis had housed themselves with their vehicles. Martin heard them talking in the garage, and at the right moment, he took a chance and ran past the garage and past Kruithof, the cigar store across from our apartment. He ran across the street, tried to open the door (normally one could stick his or her hand through the mail slot and pull the rope to unlock the door), but Pa and Moe had the door completely locked. Martin called through the mail slot, and Pa finally opened the door. How glad they were to see their oldest son alive and well with a bag of precious food. We could not wait to hear his stories of this dangerous journey.

CHAPTER 3

INSIDE OUR APARTMENT

During the last years of the war, there were always curfews, usually from 7:00 p.m. to 7:00 a.m. One could not go outside of the house or apartment during those hours; and if one did, he or she could get killed. The windows in the homes had to be darkened so that the Allies could not tell from the air where the cities were. The Nazis patrolled the streets and sometimes would shoot at windows where light was shining out. They meant what they said. "No lights shining out!" Actually, it was not much of a challenge to keep the windows dark at the end of the war because there was no electricity. At times, little candlelight in the back room was all the light we had.

When I say candlelight, I don't mean a real candle, which would have been a luxury. From a glass jelly jar, my mother and Martin made a light source by making a hole in the lid and sticking a thin, metal tube in the middle of the lid of the jar. They pushed a wick made of cloth of some sort through the tube with the bottom of the wick hanging in some oil. After lighting the top, it made a small flame that emitted just enough light to see. It also accompanied anyone to go to bathroom. Otherwise, they would have complete darkness.

All of this brings another subject to mind. It's virtually impossible to sleep for twelve hours, from 7:00 p.m. to 7:00 a.m. every day while hungry and nervous; plus, we were all cooped up in this small apartment. So what do you do as a family for all those hours when you cannot go out? There is not even enough light to read or write. This became a great bonding time for the family. Sometimes we played board games or talked of old times or imagined new times.

Pa and Moe would often tell us what we were going to do when the war ended. We would go downtown in the evening (imagine that) and see the stores because they would all be lit up. I could not imagine that because I had never seen any stores lit up at night. And Moe said that on Saturdays, we would go in the stores and buy whatever we wanted as long as we had money to pay for it—no rationing tickets, no limits on what one could buy. I just could not picture that because I did not remember what things were like before the war. We would certainly have enough food to eat, and we could go to the beach one day in the summer, to Scheveningen.

My mother, Moe, was incredible. She was very loving, industrious, ingenious, and self-sacrificing. Later in the war years, there was a shortage of everything. I recall one time when Martin, Jack, and I needed an overcoat. Winter had arrived, but no clothing stores were open. Even if they were, they had no coats. All clothing had gone to the Nazis. So Moe took one of Pa's old overcoats and made three overcoats for us. A seamstress can tell you that such is not an easy task, but she did it. I can still see her sitting at her hand-driven *Singer* sewing machine, her right hand turning the handle of the wheel, working for hours and hours, fixing things for all of us. That thing must have had a million or more miles on it.

She made underwear, hats, pants, and much more. Once, she ran short of material for undershorts for Martin and me, but she found some white and grey material. In the end, one was whitish but the other gray. And when the time came to decide who would wear the ugly, gray briefs—nobody in the world wears gray underwear—I think we drew straws. After we had gone to bed and were sound asleep, Moe, with her Dutch sense of humor, switched our underpants, and in the morning, she acted as if nothing happened. You can imagine how we felt. I remember saying, "I am sure I was wearing the other one when I went to bed." We all had a big laugh about it.

The living room in our third-floor apartment had a table surrounded by six chairs. There was no dining room, so this was a combination living/dining room. The kitchen was so small that we could not eat there. There was no room for even one chair. There was a gas stove but no refrigerator in the kitchen. We ate in the living room, and we talked in the living room. There were two larger chairs at each window corner. We never had a couch. We always sat straight up. Today, we often slouch on couches, but not then.

In the living room, there was a potbelly stove, and it was the only source of heat. As children, we got undressed in front of that stove and then ran into the bedroom to quickly get into the cold bed. In the winter, we had old towels at our feet with a warm water bottle to try to keep warm. Moe always cleaned the potbelly stove in the morning and tried to start it up again any way she could with paper, wood, coal—whatever was available—to give us some heat and a heating surface for preparing food. When the government cut off the gas, the kitchen stove was useless.

During the early part of the war, we ate meat, if available, on Sundays and Wednesdays. The other days we ate leftovers, including the gravy from the meals with meat. Only on Sunday did we get a hard-boiled egg, which came in a little eggcup. We would cut the top off and spoon out the rest piece by piece, enjoying every bit of egg.

There was no central hot water. We took a bath only once a week, when Moe could boil water to add to the cold water in the tub. We could not travel on Sundays. We could only walk to and from church, which was about forty minutes each way. We could not play outside on Sundays because the church had very strict guidelines as to what one could and could not do on the Sabbath Day. Sundays were boring for us children, especially considering that our nonreligious friends did play outside.

Besides inconveniences for our whole family, there were greater concerns for Pa who went through very difficult times personally at work, dealing with the Nazis. He was never the same after the bombardment. Apparently, his nervous system had taken a great hit. He started smoking heavily, and he had a nervous breakdown. A neurologist told Pa that he could take medication, but that the best thing for him to do was to go fishing regularly. The water can have a tranquilizing effect on one's nervous system. Pa could not follow the fishing routine because his skin was very sensitive to the sun. Big blisters would develop under his skin. I remember that vividly. He had very sensitive skin and the blisters were huge with yellow pus inside them.

One time, Pa had gone out to find some food and returned home late that night. He had bought a bag of potatoes. He got inside the door downstairs, and Moe went down the thirty-two steps to try to help him. The steps were totally dark. As Moe reached down to help Pa, she felt something soft, moist, and warm. It was Pa's eye. He was very annoyed, of course. He said, "Here I go out to try to get some food for my hungry family, and then I come home and my wife tries to poke my eye out!"

Throughout the war, Pa and Martin managed to get some food by wheeling and dealing. I remember once that some Nazi soldiers in the Ford garage near us had no cigarettes. Pa and Martin happen to have a little tobacco from which they would roll cigarettes in special, thin paper called *vloetjes*. Martin traded some of that tobacco for potatoes that day. When things got really bad, Moe traded in her wedding ring for two loaves of bread and a sack of potatoes. She also traded sheets and pillowcases for food. Some Dutch people tore down the doors inside their houses or apartments to have wood fuel for heat.

Pa often had migraine headaches, usually on Sunday afternoons, and he would say, "I am going to lie on the bed on a high pillow (*hoog kussen*)." Moe would make a headband from a rolled-up towel and put it around Pa's head, pull it as tight as she could, and tie it in the back. That seemed to give him some relief, and he could sleep for a couple of hours. Moe just plowed through everything as if nothing was ever wrong. She never complained and just kept trying to keep the morale up for the family.

Whenever any of us were sick, we called on Dr. Ver Veen. In 1944, Martin and I had *roodvonk* (scarlet fever). Apparently, I was quite sick. Dr. Ver Veen was our homeopathic physician and was wonderful. We all had the utmost confidence in him. I was the first who fell ill and pretty much had to be quarantined. Martin and Jack were not to enter my room. Martin did not. He was very careful. Jack, three years younger than me, kept running around and was exposed to me all the time. He ate from my dish; drank from my cup; and, for much of the time, he was in my room. Yet Jack did not catch the scarlet fever and Martin did.

It was toward the end of my six weeks in quarantine that Martin got sick. Dr. Ver Veen instructed us to keep an accurate record of our temperatures during this whole time, and we had to do the rectal thermometer routine twice a day. Martin seemed to have some difficulty inserting the thermometer, but I had no trouble at all. I was able to put the thermometer almost all the way in.

As a matter of fact, at one point, the thermometer disappeared completely and I could not retrieve it. What now? Unable to reach Dr. Ver Veen, Pa darted across the street to call on Dr. Du Puis. It was nighttime. The curfew was on, and the Nazis were patrolling the streets. Dr. Du Puis came, and next I was on my hands and knees in the living room on top of the table. Dr. Du Puis explained that if the glass liquid mercury thermometer would break, it could kill me. So he went to work.

After about thirty or forty minutes, Dr. Du Puis was finally able to pull the thing out. What a relief! I remember I was tired. Everyone breathed a sigh of relief, including Dr. Du Puis, who could not have taken me to the hospital at night during the curfew. I don't know if any hospital would have been ready to take on any emergencies anyway. Moe hugged me and gave me an apple. (How we got an apple then, I don't know.) I was pretty careful with the thermometer from then on.

Dr. Ver Veen also treated Pa for pleurisy. He'd tell Pa to take just a few drops of this or that. He'd keep very close track of Pa's temperature. He would predict when the fever would break, and Pa would get better. Dr. Ver Veen always seemed to be right.

When the utility company shut down and there was no gas, Moe could not cook anything on the stove in the kitchen. However, when there was electricity, she would take an electric iron, put it upside down in a bucket of sand, plug it in, and use the bottom of the iron to heat food. It might not make things boil, but it got pretty hot, and our dinner was seldom "a cold plate." Moe did the things any mother would probably do in such circumstances—anything to feed the family, clothe them, and keep them as warm as possible.

One time, Martin brought home a large sugar beet. Well, Moe knew what to do with that. She cooked part of it; served some of it raw; and from the other part, she made syrup. We had a feast on that sugar beet. Sometimes, especially during the last 1944–1945 Hunger Winter, there was no food at all. When there was even a little bit, Moe would always feed us first. She was always last. Of course, sometimes she would eat nothing at all. That's why my parents weighed about seventy-five and eighty pounds at the end of the war. We were only skin and bones and very weak.

When Moe made the syrup from the sugar beet, she hid some in a bowl high up in a kitchen cupboard. But Jack noticed it. He managed to climb up and drink all the syrup. He must have been really hungry. Moe was rather shocked when, after announcing that she had something special for all of us at dinner, she went to get the bowl and...surprise! Moe could not get too upset with this five-year-old during the Hunger Winter.

THE HUNGER WINTER

The Hunger Winter was very bad. The Dutch Government in exile had called upon the men in Holland to go on strike in "Operation Market Garden." They did, and this made Seyss-Inquart furious. He prohibited food from being transported into the area of Holland still under German control. Maastricht is in the extreme southeastern part of Holland, near Belgium, and had been liberated on September 13, 1944. This decree had particularly rigorous repercussions for Amsterdam, Rotterdam, and the Hague in the western part of the country. Rations were cut and cut again.

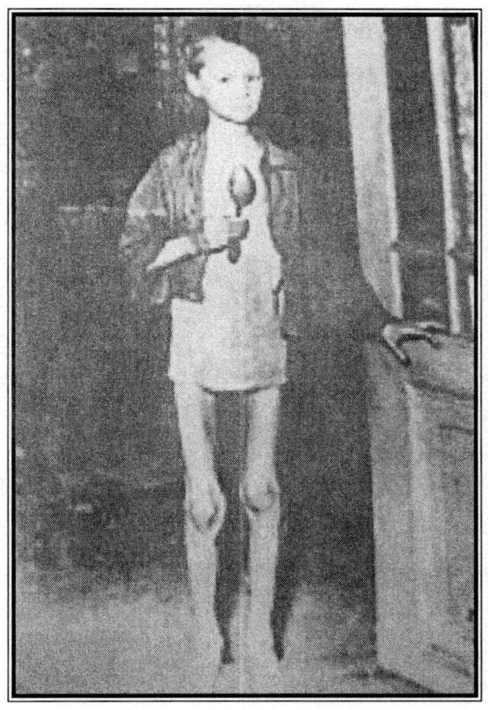

Dutch Boy undernourished

After six weeks, Seyss-Inquart rescinded his decree, and food could be brought into the cities again. But by then it was too late for many. The food situation was catastrophic. If available at all, daily food allotments were well below 450 calories. People began eating tulip bulbs and sometimes family pets. With the extreme cold, there was no electricity, wood, or running water, and sewers did not work either. Schools and factories closed. People tried to dig up streetcar and railroad tracks to get wood. People began to die, particularly the very old and the very young. The elderly froze in their unheated apartments, and children succumbed to diseases unknown to modern Holland.

Before the war, Holland was one of the best-fed and healthiest countries imaginable. But after five short years, it was one of the most miserable places on earth.

After each evening meal, whether or not there was food, Pa would read the Bible. Faithfully, he would read all or part of a chapter every day. His favorite chapter was Psalm 42. He would read with passion.

> As the deer pants for the water brooks, so pants my soul for you, O God. My soul thirsts for God, for the living God. When shall I come and appear before God? My tears have been my food day and night, while they continually say to me, "Where is your God?"
>
> Psalm 42:1–3 (NKJV)

Those war years were very dangerous times for Pa, and we did not fully realize how difficult it was for him. The notion that he might appear before God at any day was very real to him.

Moe faithfully kept a daily diary during the war years. After the war, she went through it from time to time. But when she read all the miserable experiences we had, she decided to throw the diary away. I recall her telling us that she wanted to forget and not relive all of the disappointments, the sicknesses, the fears, the uncertainties. She didn't want to experience the pain of not knowing from one day to the next whether we'd live or die, not knowing whether the next knock on the door at two or three in the morning would be the time that Pa would be arrested and taken away forever or whether we all would be killed.

She didn't want to feel the dread of wondering whether one of the many airplanes flying overhead would drop a bomb on our apartment. We were so sorry that she threw the diary away because it was full of information about the war. Her desire to do so was quite understandable, though, having lived during years of tyranny, death, starvation, and terror. It was hellish, and she just wanted to move on.

CHAPTER 4
THE HUNT FOR JEWISH PEOPLE

During the first year of the war, it became quickly obvious that the Nazis were after the Jewish people even though Israel had not invaded Germany. Although trains were scarce, the Germans somehow managed to secure some transportation of Jews from Westerbork to Auschwitz on Sunday morning, September 3, 1944, at 11:00 a.m. The train consisted of twenty-three cattle cars containing 1,109 crammed-together people like sardines, Anne Frank among them. While we were coping with day-to-day survival, the Nazis were busy hustling innocent Jewish people to concentration camps.

The Jews were forbidden to ride public transportation and could not visit places such as museums, sporting events, or theaters. They were forced to wear the yellow Jewish star on their coats for everyone to see. They could walk only on the streets by themselves, not in groups. It was as if they were leprous and had to tell everyone, as was done in Israel when someone had leprosy. For a short time, many Dutch people said, "Let's all wear the Jewish star"; but that noble thought did not last long. The Nazis were too intimidating. One could easily be arrested and/or killed.

The Nazis had incredible knowledge of who was Jewish and who was not. I vividly remember a few times when there was a knock on the downstairs door in the middle of the night, usually around two thirty in the morning. Two Nazi soldiers would come up the steps and walk all throughout our apartment to see if we were hiding any Jewish people. They did not look for weapons or any anti-Nazi literature; they were there just to see if we were hiding any Jewish people. They'd look on the roof, in all of the closets, under the beds—everywhere. On one particular night, I distinctly recall lying in bed when a huge soldier carrying a large rifle, who was wearing heavy boots and the typical Nazi helmet, looked down at me, shining his flashlight in my eyes, and then under my bed. I thought, *Is he going to kill me or all of us or just Pa?*

On one of these occasions, two Nazi soldiers were accompanied by a Dutch policeman. As the two soldiers inspected the premises, Pa began talking with the Dutch policeman.

"How are these two?"

"Well, not too bad, as it goes for Nazi soldiers."

Pa said, "This is some kind of job, going into people's homes in the middle of the night, seeing all of them in their pajamas. How long have you been doing this tonight?" He continued, "You must be hungry or thirsty. Would you like some coffee?"

"I would love some," said the Dutch policeman.

"How about those two?" Pa asked, nodding toward the Nazi soldiers.

"Well, let's ask them."

The next thing we knew, Pa asked Moe to make a pot of coffee.

"Pa, how can you do this? You want me to make coffee for the Nazis?" my mother exclaimed in disgust.

"Just make them some coffee. It will be all right," said Pa.

This scene is still carved in my memory—the living room table surrounded by the four men drinking coffee and sharing stories. Pa knew German and started asking questions. They talked very seriously. One of the Nazi soldiers had a family with three children in Germany, while the other had a family with two children. They both confessed that they did not want to be in this war. They did not want to be doing all of this.

Moe was nervous as she served coffee, careful not to touch the rifles and helmets that were parked in the corner of the living room. The men had relaxed, had become more transparent in their communications with one another, and had found that they really had a lot in common. Pa had an incredible ability to make friends, even with enemies.

After about forty-five minutes, the party broke up and they went on again to hunt for Jewish people.

In between these visits from Nazi soldiers, we had a different Nazi visit. Pa had such a way with people that he had earned the confidence of the two Nazi physicians for whom he did translation work at his government employment office. Those two physicians came to visit our apartment for tea. They even brought Moe some flowers. My mother was obviously embarrassed, and she vented her feelings openly to my father. "Pa, how can you do this? What will the neighbors think?" was Moe's logical reaction. It was a real concern for her, and a legitimate one at that. The physicians showed some class in bringing Moe flowers. Pa was hoping and praying, as Moe was, that it would never be found out how he was helping friends, relatives, and those in the Underground. (The next chapter explains Pa's role in the Underground in more detail.)

On another occasion, a team of soldiers was inspecting houses down the street from ours, and they went to an upstairs apartment. Not finding any Jewish suspects, they walked back down the steps with their heavy boots, causing dust to fall into the storage space under the steps where a Jewish family was hiding. The falling dust caused the little girl of that family to sneeze. The soldiers heard it and opened the storage space by unlocking the steps and lifting the stairway. The father, mother, and children were immediately taken away, never to be seen again. They most likely wound up in a concentration camp in Germany. This was the war picture: a totally innocent family taken away to be killed. How terribly cruel this was as well as drastic, unjust, and hateful. The Nazis had near zero compassion.

Downstairs at our address, Bergweg 141, there was a storefront that was operated by Mr. and Mrs. Van Leeuwen. He was a shoemaker, and he and his wife were very quiet, private people. My parents just had a casual relationship with them. He repaired our shoes, belts, and other things over the years. My parents did not know they were Jewish, but the Nazis did. One morning, we found out that they had been taken away during the night, and we never saw them again.

Martin remembers that a Polish girl, Rosa Slamovitz, and her family were taken away. She suddenly was missing from Martin's class in school. The Nazis had found out that she was Jewish and took her away.

The Dutch were known for being very supportive of the Jews and Jewish causes, very pro-Semitic, which is a word one does not hear very often. Martin told me, however, of one exception. There was a man, Mr. de Mats, who lived across the street from us, and he had purchased something from the Geleski family. This elderly Jewish couple lived in a small apartment rented from Tom van Outgaarden, Martin's friend. Tom had a photography studio down the street from us. The man, Mr. de Mats, very sadly refused to pay and had taken the attitude that the Geleskis were "just a couple of Jews" and would most likely be taken away anyway. Well, they were.

Here was a retired Jewish couple, eking out a living on a small pension, minding their own business, trying to be good Dutch citizens, undoubtedly having no political ambitions, and feeling helpless against a potential Nazi threat. They probably got little to no help or advice from their synagogue, if it was open and functioning at all. There was a knock on their door at 3:00 a.m. one morning, waking them from a sound sleep. We don't know what really happened, what they were told, whether they changed from their pajamas to regular street clothes, or whether or not they were given time to gather personal belongings.

We do know that they were suddenly and brutally extracted from their apartment and whisked away in a Nazi vehicle. Why? They were of Jewish ancestry. How horrible, unreasonable, and atrocious. And all because one man, Adolf Hitler, decided this must be done. Who told him to do this? It was obviously not God. We were ashamed of people like Mr. de Mats and felt quite sorry for him. We don't know whether or not Mr. de Mats reported the Geleski family to the Nazis. Perhaps their names and those of other Jewish people were obtained from the Dutch census bureau.

The United Nations has documented human rights violations around the world, and the barbaric exterminations of Jewish citizens and others were recorded as extreme violations of human rights. Jewish people suffered everywhere under Hitler.

As the German army collapsed, the Second U.S. Calvary, led by Col. Charles Reed, was approaching Flossenburg with other elements of the Third Army, commanded by Gen. George S. Patton, the army in which my wife's uncle, Bryan Dorn, served.[7] The Nazi SS guards and a column of about five hundred prisoners from Flossenburg arrived on April 21, 1945, in a death march through Neunburg, a small town in Germany. The local citizens wanted to help the prisoners as they passed right in front of them, but the SS guards blocked them. The citizens were not allowed to feed the starving and worn-out prisoners. In that same area, around the Demi farm, ten prisoners died before the night was over. The SS were brutal. The next morning, some 161 prisoners were found dead along the sides of the road they had traveled. Some were buried in shallow graves.

Once the Americans arrived at the scene, they assessed the situation. They ordered the shallow graves to be opened in order for the dead to be re-buried in a proper grave, with markers, to achieve a sense of dignity. The dead were Polish, Hungarian, Romanian, and Yugoslavian. All of them were Jews. It was a ghastly sight. The American commanders decided to help those German citizens understand what they were seeing. They held the citizens responsible, not just for the murders in their area, but for all of the sins of Hitler's Germany. Some people did not understand, trying to say that it was not their fault, but most understood that it was. Isn't it an interesting concept, to hold individual citizens responsible for the actions of their government? Does your vote count? You bet it does.

After quickly assembling coffins, the Americans made the German citizens carry the dead to a burying place. The citizens were made to watch and participate. What a picture. Most never forgot, and most agree with the action taken by the Americans.

CHAPTER 5

PA AND THE UNDERGROUND

There was a lot of unemployment at the beginning of the war. Pa was working for the Dutch government at the employment office in Rotterdam. His specialty was to find employment for handicapped and disabled people, and he was very good at that. But he also found jobs for others, like my Uncle Jan, Moe's brother, who was able to get a position as a streetcar conductor in Rotterdam.

From 1942 on, the Nazis made a decree that any Dutchman, age eighteen to forty-five, was eligible to work in German factories. In small groups, those men were called up from the labor statistics records of Holland—in our case, Rotterdam—and they were notified to come to the employment office at Middelland Straat, where Pa worked. Each man was called in to appear before a Nazi physician, and his papers were checked, and he was questioned about his health. The physician would then decide if the man had any diseases that would disqualify him from being transported to Germany. Most Dutchmen did not speak German, and my father was assigned to interpret for the Nazi physician. Pa noticed that certain problems such as bedwetting, mental problems (or even the suspicion of such), and other ailments would disqualify people.

At the end of each day, my father would stack the documents for the examined men, and the physician would sign each form at the lower right-hand corner. This became so habitual that the doctor, who began to trust Pa, would just fold over the lower right-hand corner of each page and sign without looking at the whole form. At this point, every once in awhile, Pa would take a great risk and slip in a blank form, which would also receive the doctor's signature. Pa would use that form and fill in the names of any Underground friends, family, or relatives in order to keep the husbands, the breadwinners, from being transported to Germany.

This was very important to Pa. He knew how hard it was for any family to survive, to gather food and fuel supplies, without the man of the house present. Pa never knew if anyone would find out what he was doing. Sometimes he was more afraid of his coworkers than of the enemy. It was not uncommon for some Dutch people to become traitors just to survive. It was tempting when things were going poorly. Under dire circumstances such as these, a man with the responsibility of his family could be tempted to do the unthinkable—turn into a traitor. Therefore, when a knock on the door came in the middle of the night, Pa never knew whether it was for him or whether they were looking for Jewish people. I know of at least two occasions when Pa thought his plot had been uncovered and he would be arrested. He said good-bye to us and gave Moe last-minute instructions.

Moe suffered quietly, pondering all these things in her heart. She prayed quite a lot. One can only imagine what goes on in a mother's heart.

Another method used in Pa's office was to burn some of the doctor's forms in the office's potbelly stove. Some of Pa's coworkers were aware of that. There was one occasion when a man had received notice to appear before the Nazi doctor but decided not to show up. A couple of weeks later, he had second thoughts and did appear, explaining why he did not come and that he was now ready to be examined for work in Germany. He was examined, but the doctor did not like his initial refusal and put a note in an envelope stating that he was not to be trusted and should be "taken care of" by the authorities. This was, in effect, his death sentence.

The man was told to take the envelope with him and present it to his superiors once he arrived in Germany. Pa knew what was in the note and chased the man to his house, spoke with him, and even had trouble convincing him that he was carrying his own death sentence. But finally he agreed to the truth and went into hiding with the Underground and apparently survived.

My brothers and I, of course, did not know that anything like this was going on. Pa kept everything a secret. It was not until after the war that I found out, but not because Pa told me. When I was with Pa downtown in Rotterdam at some public event, like a soccer game, every once in a while someone would come up to Pa and thank him for keeping a family member from having to go to Germany. Very grateful people gave Pa an emotional thank you. So I questioned Pa about these people thanking him, and the story finally came out.

Another aspect of this was that in the beginning, the Germans had *a real* program for Dutch people to work in German factories where war machinery was produced. As he was sometimes assigned to supervise the transport of groups of men to the German factories, Pa had been to Germany to see these facilities. Pa found out that this was *real.* The men actually worked under conditions that were not bad. They got paid, had decent living quarters, and were fed and treated well. So when he was back in Holland, he told the workers that the situation for them would not be too bad and described it for them. Most of the men wondered if they would be taken to concentration camps instead of factories. But when Pa tried to convince them of the truth, some suspected Pa of being on the German side. This was understandable, but sometimes it put Pa in some very difficult situations.

At any rate, he apparently helped quite a few people. He managed to keep all five of his brothers out of Germany, except his younger brother, Jacob. No matter how he tried to avoid deportation, Jacob had to go. Once in Germany, Jacob started coughing and was sent to the hospital, where a Dutch physician saw him. After some tests, it was determined that he had to go back to Holland immediately. What a relief for Pa. He loved all of his brothers, especially Jacob.

During the last year of the war, the Nazis launched V-1 and V-2 bomb missiles. They were aimed at England, but some fell short. Quite a few went over Rotterdam on the way to their destination. Two bombs fell near us, one on a couple of houses on the Liststraat, which was two to three minutes away from where we lived. Two houses were totally flattened, killing everyone inside. I saw it with my own eyes, and it left quite an imprint on my mind.

Also in 1944, Allied forces mistakenly dropped some bombs on West Rotterdam. It happened twice, and the second time, we sat at the bottom of the steps, ready to run out in case a bomb fell on us. Whenever any airplanes approached Rotterdam, the sirens would go off. Everyone knew what these sirens meant: bombs could fall, and airplanes could be shot down or crash-land on any houses. The sirens alone were quite frightening to me. Life could end for any of us at any time.

The best place for us to be in our any building was right behind the front door, and in our case, at the bottom of our thirty-two steps, so we would be ready to run out into the street should our apartment building collapse. We would huddle behind the front door with some belongings, just waiting. Sometimes we'd hear the whistling of descending bombs, and we'd wait for the explosion. Who would be hit next? Would it be us or someone else? Of course, the city was totally dark at night due either to the curfew, other restrictions, or because there was no electricity at all. Afterward, there was a single siren announcing that the danger had passed and we could all go back upstairs.

CHAPTER 6
THE RAZZIAS

Throughout the war, the Nazis conducted *razzias* (roundups) in Holland. In other parts of the country, they started as early as 1942. In Rotterdam, they started in 1944. The Nazis would suddenly go into a neighborhood, cordon off the area, and go into each home to look for any males between seventeen and forty-two. When they came to our area, Nazis with machine guns blocked everything off at 8:00 a.m. Everyone was told that at 11:00 a.m. all males between seventeen and forty-two were to step outside and line up in the middle of the street.

The Nazis entered our apartment, checked Pa and Martin's birth certificates, and were we ever blessed! Pa and Martin missed the cut-off on both sides. Pa was forty-four, and Martin was fifteen. At eleven o'clock, there was a long line of men in the middle of the Bergweg on the streetcar tracks with machine gun-carrying soldiers astride them. It did not matter if they were healthy or not, bedwetters, or mentally disabled; they all had to go.

Can you imagine what this was like—all male neighbors in any neighborhood being marched off, possibly to death? They did not know how long they would be gone or whether they would ever see their loved ones again. Think of your own street and neighborhood today. What if an enemy were to invade the United States and round up all of your male neighbors one morning to take them away forever? So many families would be without the breadwinner, the man of the home. But that's precisely what happened in Rotterdam and in other cities in Holland.

I do remember that Martin and I did not feel very sorry for one man in the line. He was a local policeman who had, on a number of occasions, taken away our paper soccer ball when we tried to play around the corner on the Willebrordersplein. (How cruel we can be as children.) Normal soccer balls had not been available for quite a while, so we made balls from newspaper and tightly wound them with rubber bands. It worked pretty well.

Martin had some fine friends who bonded during the war. Sjaak Braams, Tom van Outgaarden, Jan Hezemans, Joop de Molt, and Lo de Vos stand out in my memory. Nico van Vliet, with whom I went to school, was my friend. Martin's friends and I played soccer around the corner whenever we could. Though those boys had some fun together, they also worked hard to get food and fuel for their families during the war.

Martin wanted to join the active Underground, but he was too young. It was too dangerous. The Underground was very active and took many risks to save people's lives.

Moe told Jack of an instance where Martin, who was at the ambachtschool, a trade school, walked into an office at the school without knocking. Martin faced a group of men who had drawn their guns and aimed them at him. Pa was one of those men. It was a meeting of the Underground. If a Nazi had walked in, they would have killed him right then and there.

I also recall that a British Royal Air Force fighter plane was shot down and crash-landed in a square in the middle of Rotterdam. The pilot survived and got out of the plane. Soon afterward, the Nazis surrounded the plane, but the pilot had already been taken away by the Underground. The pilot was then hidden in various homes, being frequently moved to a different location during the night, and he survived the war. Most of the Underground managed to escape the *razzias* so they could do what needed to be done to help the Dutch and fight the Nazis.

CRAZY TUESDAY

On September 5, 1944, when the Allies had taken Antwerp in Belgium, the Dutch were told that freedom would come any minute, and then Dolle Dinsdag, or Crazy Tuesday, happened. This occurred when the Dutch people heard over the BBC Radio from England that the Allied Forces were very close, near Dordrecht, some twenty kilometers away on the way from Rotterdam. People put flags out to welcome the troops, and excitement was building in the neighborhood. But the report turned out to be erroneous. We had been through that sort of thing before. The Nazis put a quick stop to that, arresting some and shooting others.

Rien, Joop, and Jan (Martin, Jack, and John), 1940

The NSB (the National Socialistic Movement, pro-Nazi) was quite concerned, because if Holland was freed, what would happen to them? So a great exodus of NSB members was seen as they and their families tried desperately to flee to Germany. Public transportation was now largely inoperative, and many of those people went on foot.

After the invasion of Normandy on June 6, 1944, rumors floated around again that the Allies were getting very close. In reality, the winter of 1944–45 was still ahead. This was also called the "Hunger Winter" which, fortunately, was not quite as bitterly cold as usual.

CHAPTER 7

THE LAST PUSH TOWARD FREEDOM

By April 1945, spring had come and with it some warmer weather. The food situation remained very acute. Liberation, which once seemed so close, now seemed so far away. If something did not happen soon, there would be mass starvation in Holland. Food supplies were now virtually exhausted. On April 29, 1945, Canadian troops began pouring into the northern provinces. Next to Norway, Holland was the country to be occupied by the Germans the longest.

In the course of this war, some two hundred thousand people lost their lives in Holland. One hundred thousand of them were Jewish. Some sixteen thousand died during the Hunger Winter. Thirty thousand Dutch people died in concentration camps for having been involved in anti-German activities. In Holland, two thousand were executed for such activities. During Operation Market Garden, when the Dutch went on strike, some two thousand died in the city of Arnhem. The movie *A Bridge Too Far* depicts, quite accurately, what happened. Field Marshall Montgomery had been warned by the Dutch Underground that there was a whole German Panzer division in Arnhem. They were there resting up before being sent to Russia. Montgomery did not believe the report, and the operation failed badly. The Nazis intercepted the airlifted supplies, including cigarettes, and they laughed at the unexpected blessings from the sky.

Earlier in the war, Winston Churchill had been busy trying to get President Roosevelt to commit to the European war theater. Churchill and Roosevelt met on the deck of the British Battleship, *HMS Prince of Wales*, on August 10-12, 1941. The Atlantic Charter Conference was held in Placentia Bay, Newfoundland. Roosevelt arrived on the *USS McDougal.*

In the photo, Roosevelt and Churchill are seated, and standing behind them are Admiral Ernest J. King, USN (between Roosevelt and Churchill); General George C. Marshall, US Army; General Sir John Dill, British Army; and others. At far left is Harry Hopkins, talking with W. Averall Harriman. In the photo of the ship with all the sailors, one can see the two world leaders sitting just beyond the tip of the left cannon.

The photos were taken during the church service held on the deck of the Prince of Wales. What an awesome sight as the all-navy crew/choir/congregation sang with Churchill and Roosevelt. The clergy can be seen on the right.

It is most unusual to have such a large church service on the deck of a huge naval vessel in the North Atlantic during a war. They all were unified in singing "Onward Christian Soldiers, Marching as to war, With the cross of Jesus, Going on before..." I understand they sang all five stanzas. This could have been of great spiritual significance, as it might have been a turning point or perhaps *the* turning point of the war.

What a difference compared to the other side, where Hitler was shouting, "*Deutschland uber alles*"—Germany above (or over) everything, without God, of course. Who was on God's side?

During the war, each New Year's Eve, we would sit in the living room and talk about the past year and wonder if this would be our last New Year's Eve. Five times, things had gotten worse—in 1941, 1942, 1943, 1944, and 1945. The food shortages, the diseases, the number of neighbors taken away or killed, and then the false rumors all had added up to an increasingly dim picture. *Would this war ever come to an end?* We were all really nearly facing certain death. We just did not know when, where, and how.

Atlantic Charter Conference, August 1941, church service on the after deck of *HMS Prince of Whales*

Atlantic Charter Conference, August 1941, Roosevelt and Churchill

The uncertainties gnawed at our souls and minds and bodies. We all were hungry too, of course. Except through prayer and the hope that the Allies would deliver us, there was no relief in sight. The Allies seemed to be inching toward us, but would they really come through? All these thoughts would come to a head on New Year's Eve. At twelve o'clock, Pa would stand up and go over to Moe and just hug her, both crying, sobbing. It was extremely emotional. We would join them, taking turns hugging one another and crying tears of shared grief.

Another year was born. Would it be a year of more grief, disease, and possible death for any of us, especially Pa? Or would next year's New Year's Eve be a better one? Actually, the more accurate thought we all had was: will we see each other again at all next year at this time?

In various ways, my father and Martin tried to keep up with the progress of the war. Martin had a map of Western Europe on the wall in our room, and he placed a little flag on each town conquered by the Allies. Thus, ever so slowly, we saw them coming closer. He got information from some Underground contact, and Pa got information from a Roman Catholic priest. This priest had hidden a radio in the eaves of his parish church, way up near the peak of the roof. He would climb up there each morning and listen to the BBC from London to get the latest news.

The Nazis had confiscated all radios during the first weeks of the war. We had a government radio. Hilversum I and II were the two radio stations we always listened to. In the first two weeks of the war, those stations went off the air, and it was strictly forbidden to have any other radio. So after the priest heard the BBC news, he would take a walk to meet Pa on the sidewalk near our apartment, only three blocks away from the church. Then the priest and Pa would just casually walk side by side, sharing the news of that day. It was a pretty neat arrangement, and the enemy never found out.

That priest also hid some Jewish people in his parish as my father later did. Pa and his brother, Cornelius, hid some twenty-five Jewish people under the large pulpit of our church during the last few months of the war. Uncle Cornelius was the trustee or caretaker of the church, and his house was located next door on church property. Pa's job was to feed the Jewish families, and Uncle Cornelius's job was to keep them safe and quiet. There were children amongst them. It was tough to keep them from crying while people were in the church on Sunday morning or at any other time. At times, when the church was empty, they were let out so they could visit the bathroom and walk around a little. Of course, this was a top secret project. I don't know who had the toughest job. Food was extremely scarce, and security was a life or death situation for all involved.

FINALLY, FREEDOM FROM TYRANNY

The end of the war was an event I cannot ever possibly forget. It was a sunny morning on May 5, 1945, and there were strong rumors that the Allied troops were getting very close. We did not know how close, though, and we had heard many rumors before, always with disappointing results. Martin had gone out with his longtime friend from school, Sjaak Braams, to check if there was any truth to these rumors. At about ten o'clock, he came running upstairs to tell us he had seen an American car going by out front. We said, "Sure. How do you know it was an American car?" Well, Martin described a green car, a military car, but instead of a swastika painted on the side, there was a white star on the door. That was pretty convincing to us, so we looked out the window, and indeed,soon after that, the same car went by, going the other way. It was a green Jeep with a white star on the side. It was probably a patrol car scouting the area to make sure all was safe. Excitement filled the air.

I saw people running, some carrying flags. I thought that was dangerous because on Crazy Tuesday I had seen people carrying flags, and some were arrested and shot by the Nazis, who quickly brought that day under control. Could that happen again, another false alarm? It was a beautiful, sunny day. I went downstairs and just stood at the edge of the sidewalk, trying to determine what was happening. Martin ran to his friends. As I was standing there, I began to hear a rumbling sound coming from my left, from the east, and suddenly I saw the front of a big, green army truck coming around the corner and behind it another truck and then a big tank.

As they came closer, I saw that on these trucks with white stars on the sides, and in those tanks were soldiers, also in green uniforms; but these soldiers were smiling and waving. I had seen a lot of soldiers in the last five years, but they never smiled as far as I could recall. But these people were friendly. As the tanks and trucks rumbled by, I began shaking, partly from the ground shaking underfoot from the heavy vehicles riding right in front of me, partly from excitement, and partly from weakness.

I don't know how much or how little I weighed, but I know I was weak. These soldiers were bringing us freedom. That's all I knew. In my life, up to that point, I had only known enemy occupation. Now I sensed an exhilarating feeling of real joy, peace, and freedom being brought right to our doorstep. It was so exciting, uplifting, momentous, life changing.

It became difficult to take it all in. It was like going from hell to heaven. I remember thinking, *Is this real? Can this really be happening?* But it was very real. These wonderful soldiers in those trucks were real. These tanks and trucks with white stars on their sides were different from what I had ever seen. Suddenly I saw Martin with a couple of his friends, very excited, running from tank to truck, touching American soldiers' hands, just beaming with happiness. Then I saw Martin and one of his friends on top of one of the tanks, waving and screaming with joy.

Most people living in freedom often do not appreciate freedom until it is taken away from them. Then, when the taste of freedom comes again, it is really welcomed with great enthusiasm and super, inner joy. Of course, Pa and Moe came out as well, and they were so delighted with that great day. A lot of people cried from happiness, as did Pa and Moe. Finally, finally, freedom had really come.

I remember going with Martin to the Lisplein (Lis Square) a few blocks away, where the American and Canadian troops had stopped to set up camp for the night. Martin spoke with a number of these wonderful, freedom-bringing heroes and invited some to our apartment. That evening, three Canadian soldiers came upstairs to visit us, bringing cookies with them, and we shared a wonderful time together. I remember I did not say much. I did not speak any English, and I was just trying to soak it all in. What a change of events. I recall the smell of the uniforms of the Americans and Canadians, their boots, their belts, their confident, and pleasant personalities. These people were wonderful. What different sensations I felt compared to the Nazi soldiers. Apparently, Pa and Moe's prayers really had been answered.

The war left Holland devastated, especially due to the events that transpired in the last six months. The Nazis tried to forestall the Allies and blew up the great harbor facilities of Rotterdam and Amsterdam, as well as miles and miles of train tracks. They blew up many Dutch dikes, flooding thousands of acres of land. Although the task of rebuilding seemed insurmountable, rebuild they did, with much help from the American Marshall Plan.

Of course, right after the war ended, there was still a lot of hunger and shortages of all kinds. It took a good while for food to arrive from various sources. I do remember, just prior to the end of the war, some Allied planes flying over to drop bags of food in certain areas around Rotterdam. Seyss-Inquart had agreed to a plan that would allow the Allies to airlift food supplies to starving Holland. When the bags fell out of the sky, Martin would go with his friends and grab as much as they could. They would stuff their pants full with a few cans and packages of food before the Nazis came to chase them away. Some soldiers had not heard of Seyss-Inquart's approval. Overall, it was a small amount of food, but still it was a relief from going hungry. It was mostly K-rations such as chocolate, food bars, crackers, etc. It was wonderful. Martin came home one day with some peanuts. My father told us how wonderful peanuts are and how rich in food value they are. I tried one but did not like it at all—too dry and crunchy without taste. Well, Pa straightened me out quickly and showed me I should peel them and then eat the nuts on the inside. Imagine. I was almost nine years old and did not know how to eat a peanut. I had never seen one. I had never seen a banana either. Slowly but surely, different foods did start to come in.

Very soon after the war, Pa's brother-in-law, Uncle Bram van Bochove, invited me to spend a couple of weeks at his house. He had a grocery store in South Rotterdam, which was empty, of course. Uncle Bram knew our family was in great need of some food, any food. The Swedish government had sent some shipments of white bread, milk, and butter to Rotterdam. To insure fair and equitable distribution, the Swedish food was distributed through various neighborhood stores, and Uncle Bram's was assigned as one of those.

I remember coming in and meeting a policeman in the store. He spent the night there because there was the real danger of some extremely desparate hungry people breaking in to get to the food. The bread and dairies had arrived that evening, and distribution would start the next morning. Uncle Bram was allowed a very small amount for himself and the family, so he invited us on the evening before distribution. I still remember that we were seated around the table—Uncle Bram and Aunt Greta with Marien, their son who was about my age, and his older sister, Nel.

Uncle Bram said a special thanksgiving prayer, and I received a slice of real white bread with a good amount of butter spread on it and some white sugar sprinkled on top of the butter. I can still smell it and certainly taste it. I put my teeth in that slice of bread with butter and sugar and had never tasted anything so delicious. It was the best bite of food I had had in a long, long time.

Another vivid experience I had was when our church had arranged with some farmers in the southern part of Holland to host some undernourished children from the city. I was sent to one of those farms. What a tremendous experience for a city kid. I got to eat great food and drink fresh milk. I met amazing people, got to ride in a horse and buggy, helped care for the cows and horses and chickens, etc. I remember going with the farmer to bring in the cows in the evening. We'd get inside the fence at a meadow, and he'd call the cows in. Some cows were not so obedient and stayed all the way at the other end of the pasture. So we had to go and "encourage" them. I would talk to the cows and grab the tail of one and as the cow started running toward the farmer, I'd run behind it and let it pull me "home." What an experience that was!

I also got to wear real wooden shoes. They were hard to get used to, but after a while, I could run in them. The smell of the barn was wonderful, breathtaking (literally), and not unpleasant at all; and to sit on top of the carriage looking down on the galloping horses when I could go with the farmer to downtown was very exciting. It was as if a whole new world had opened up to me, and I guess it had.

Even though the Dutch had abolished the death penalty in 1860, after the war they briefly introduced it again and executed some of the most blatant collaborationists. Anton Mussert, the NSB head, and Seyss-Inquart were both executed by a firing squad in Holland.

In our neighborhood, some girls whom the Underground knew to have sympathized with the Nazi soldiers and/or officers, some having provided sexual services as well, were rounded up. Around the corner, on the Willebrordersplein, there was a fallout shelter that was built up to a sort of a hill in the middle of the square. Those girls were placed on a chair on top of the shelter, hands tied behind their backs, and their hair was shaved till they were bald. Then the Underground painted a swastika on the top of their heads with black tar, and they were forced to sing a song that went like this: "*Kale, kale kop, met een hagenkruis op top*," or "Bald, bald head, with a swastika on top." I believe they were also forced to sing the Dutch national anthem. Of course, a large crowd gathered to see the spectacle, and, indeed, it was humiliating for those girls, but all felt they were quite deserving of it. They could have been executed for treason as well.

Anton Mussert (Please note the cover of this book)

Some others were sentenced to help rebuild the infrastructure. By 1952, seven years later, Holland had virtually completed the rebuilding of the country, as I mentioned before, with much assistance from the American Marshall Plan. So the Nazis and their sympathizers were on the oppressors' side, the destroyers' side, while the patriotic, normal, and usually Christian Dutch citizens were on the moral side, which builds up and does not tear down or kill.

Christ taught that the norm for the true Christian is the exertion of some moral influence on society. This is defined as "salt" to the culture: "You are the salt of the earth." (Matthew 5:13a NKJV).

PART II

FREEDOM

CHAPTER 8

WHAT NOW, AFTER THE WAR?

After the war was over, my parents began taking us downtown on Saturdays. In particular, one visit stands out: a stop at the Poffertjeskraam. This was a very popular attraction where silver dollar pancakes (Poffertjes) were made in front of your eyes, and you could eat them at an outdoor café-type setup. I still remember the sounds at the stand and the wonderful smell of those small pancakes. There was a chef in his white outfit and the high chef's hat who was kept very busy trying to keep up with the orders.

After five years of being hungry, this was a real delight. The chef was very apt at pouring the batter into the molds, and once one side was done, he took a fork and very quickly flipped each pancake down the row to bake the other side. We were just fascinated by that. Then, when it was time to devour these delicacies covered with butter and white powdered sugar, we just slowly took the dish to a table and sat there in the open air, thoroughly enjoying each bite of this delightful treat, very much regretting there was no more after the last bite.

The atmosphere surrounding us was very happy, peaceful, and exciting. The smiling faces expressed a deep and long-awaited joy and sweet satisfaction. This was the opposite feeling of the great hunger we had experienced. A new, peaceful world had opened up to us, and it was very satisfying to take it all in. Again, it was like having been through a sort of hell for the past five years and finding ourselves in a heavenly atmosphere. The experience said, Rotterdam is back again! Thank God!

After the war, a monument, shown in the photo, served as a

reminder of what happened. The creator of the monument was Ossip Zadkine, a French/Russian sculptor, who depicted Rotterdam with the heart missing because the center of the city had been flattened by the 1940 bombardment. It's called "The Destroyed City" and sometimes called "The City without a Heart."

Statue depicting "The City without a Heart"

As I explained earlier, we were privileged to spend time on different farms so as to gain some weight and get our strength back. Other experiences followed: Jack and I went to Meppen in Drente, and Martin went to Terneuzen with the Dekker family. Soon after those trips, Jack and I went to a farm in Numansdorp in the province of Zeeland. Moe took us to Zuidplein (South Square) in South Rotterdam, where we boarded a steam train that took us to a boat, which, in turn, took us slowly on a six- to eight-hour journey to Numansdorp. There we were again as city boys in a foreign environment with cows, horses, chickens, and other animals, and we loved it. The adjustment was not hard. We ate wonderful food and enjoyed helping. When the farmer was hired to do a wedding or a funeral with his horse and buggy, we had fun riding with him. It was a marvelous change for us.

Jack and I also recall that one of the farmer's sons later came to visit us in Rotterdam. His name was Kees. We went on a streetcar to see downtown Rotterdam and explained to him that you had to buy a ticket. Now, a child up to age eleven could get a ticket for six cents, but at age twelve and above, one had to pay ten cents. There were two conductors on each streetcar. One drove, and the other collected the money. He had a small metal dispenser on his belt from which he dispensed the ticket as he took the money. When confronted by the conductor, we explained to Kees about the ticket. Kees and I were between ten and eleven years of age, so we qualified for the six-cent ticket, which I recommended. But no. Kees wanted a "big" ticket. I told him he did not have to do that, but he said because he was now in the big city he wanted a "big" ticket. The conductor just smiled and gave him the ten-cent ticket. I had trouble understanding Kees' rationale.

I have very fond memories of the Dutch streetcars. We used them frequently because the public transportation system in Holland was excellent, as it still is today. The highway signs are also outstanding. It's hard to get lost there.

As a boy, whenever I got on a streetcar in Holland, I always darted right to the front to stand next to the conductor-driver. I was fascinated by all the handles, buttons, emergency gadgets, and the whole prospect of seeing him speed up and slow down to pick up passengers. At one time, I wanted to become one of them. Most drivers were friendly. At night, the conductor would draw a curtain around himself so as to not be disturbed by the bright lights from behind him, which reflected on the front, flat window. I would always try to get inside the curtain with him to see everything. Most of the time, he would let me in.

Just as there was a great surge of patriotism in the United States after 9/11, so was there such a surge in Holland after World War II. It affected our family because it was this real sense of Dutch patriotism that caused Martin to sign on with the Royal Dutch Navy. He went through a year or so of basic training and then was assigned to do duty on a naval vessel.

I still vividly remember that Pa called for a Ravero taxi (which was a very special thing because we hardly ever rode in a taxi) to take us all to the Rotterdam train station to see Martin off to Den Helder, in the north of Holland, where he had been assigned to the Navy Destroyer, *HMS Kortenaar* (*Her Majesty's Ship*). It was a very somber morning for us all. We did not know how long he would be gone, but it would be at least one year to Indonesia, which was still called the Netherlands East Indies at that time.

We all loved Martin. He was such a big part of the family through the very difficult war years. He would often bring the latest news, and when we were badly in need, he would surprise us with food or fuel. He was brave, daring, and adventurous.

We had become such a close-knit family that it was very difficult to see Martin leave us so dramatically. We did not want to be without him, and I especially did not want to see him go. I admired him so much. He was my hero. I was proud of the fact that he had patriotically joined the navy. I loved the smell of his uniform when he came home on the weekends. I was seven years younger. He was my big brother, who would protect me if I were in trouble. I looked up to him as I looked up to my father.

I loved his navy stories he told us when he was home for the weekend. He was on one small navy vessel when, one day, one by one, the men in his group were called to the captain's office. They had no idea for what reason. As each man came back to the mess hall, all the others asked what it was all about. Each one would say, "I didn't know what the captain was talking about. I didn't do it."

"Well, what did he say?"

"I don't know. You'll find out when you see him."

By the time the last one had to go in, he was really nervous, thinking he must be the one suspected of something horrible. It turned out that they all had been promoted, and each caught on to what the previous one pretended. When the last one came back to the mess hall, they all just burst out laughing.

Another typical navy men's story was that they would each be drinking a glass of something—be it a beer or a soda—and when one was called out of the room, where he could not take the drink with him, he would put a note next to his glass to protect his drink, which said, "I've spit in this." When he would come back, there'd be an additional comment, which said, "We did too."

Martin always had a great sense of humor, and it made him a popular, happy man. He has always been this way. I recall that, years later, when we lived in Baltimore, Pa became ill and had to go to the local hospital emergency room. Jack, Martin, and I were with Pa by ourselves as we waited for the doctor to return. Waiting in an emergency room can take on a life of its own. After we had been there awhile and we had gone through the usual small talk, Martin finally said, "Well, Pa, it's not so bad here. Look, Jack will come to see you this coming Christmas, I'll come and see you next Christmas, and John the Christmas after that!" How encouraging. We all had a good laugh, especially Pa. Although Pa and Moe are no longer with us, and Martin passed away in January 2009, we were and still are a close family.

It was so difficult to let Martin go so far away. As it turned out, his one-year trip to Indonesia became two years and then three and finally three and a half years. Those were very difficult years for Martin. He was a machinist, working in the engine room, of course, but the ship was not air-conditioned, and they were in the tropics. The whole ship was hot, especially the engine room. There, the men had to take salt tablets all the time to replace salt lost by perspiration. We did not get much mail from Martin's ship, but when some mail did come, we devoured the latest news.

One time, there was a letter with a wonderful surprise for me. Martin sent a check for 141 guilders so Pa and Moe could take me to the bicycle shop and purchase a brand-new bicycle. What a day that was. I still remember it. There I was, getting to choose a brand-new bicycle for myself. I chose a Phoenix bicycle. What a thrill that was for me. Martin knew I had wanted a bike for a long time, but we could not afford one. In the meantime, I had a little old, red scooter. The new bike, however, was black and shiny, with beautiful tires—just gorgeous. Martin did not have much money at all because his navy pay was meager. But he saved up 'till he could send me that surprise. What a brother.

A gorgeous new bike, a great gift from my big brother.

My parents never owned a car and really did not need one because the streetcar came right by our apartment and stopped in front of Nico van Vliet's father's grocery store about fifteen doors away. I suppose that if they had the money, they might have bought a car; but such was not the case.

My family had been through so much together during the war. We had a wonderful relationship, but my attraction to America eventually became so strong in my mind that it overcame the formidable strength of the bond with my family. It was a very emotional tug of war within me. I did not want to break my mother's heart by leaving her, and to leave would break my heart as well. Here we had been through five years of fear that the Nazis would break up our family, and now I wanted to do the same thing. But I had to find out where these wonderful people came from. And I had to find out why the Americans were the way they were, being able to extend freedom to other countries. I did realize that one could possibly make more money in America than in Holland, but that was not my dominant thought. I did not have a plan to pursue any particular vocation, business, or profession. In my subconscious, I believed God had put this vision in my mind for me to see America; and once that was accomplished, he would show me what to do.

Pa was a hard worker, as was Moe. Pa survived World War II, helped quite a few people escape from being transported to Germany, helped the Dutch Underground, hid Jewish people, and provided for and protected his family, all with God's help.

Pa Vandenberge

To taste freedom after being in bondage for five long years was a glorious, much appreciated experience. People started to make plans again. It took quite a while for the excitement to die down. I recall that there was a Dutch comedian on the radio one Saturday night—never heard a comedian during the war, of course—who made a very interesting, comical comment after the Dutch National Soccer team had played against the Germans a couple of years after the war in Germany.

The Dutch team won 2–1, and his take on it was, "See what happens when they only come with just eleven!" (instead of a big army). I also recall another very happy moment when it was announced that Sir Winston Churchill, escorted by Queen Wilhelmina, was coming to Holland to visit Rotterdam. I went to city hall on my bike and found a huge crowd of enthusiastic, patriotic Dutch people who admired Churchill greatly. They were cheering, and as I got closer, our Queen appeared on the second-floor balcony with Sir Winston Churchill, who waved to the crowd his famous "V-sign" with one hand while holding his cigar in the other. I don't think there was any speech, at least I don't remember one; but just being there and seeing him was just wonderful. It gave me courage, hope, determination, and a strong desire to make the best out of this new future. As a youngster, it was extremely exciting for me.

Something major had happened to my mind and my spirit during the Liberation. Seeing the Americans come and give us freedom was so very big that I believe God put a desire, a goal, or a vision in the back of my head. I could not get rid of it. Not that I wanted to, but it dominated my thinking so much that no one could talk me out of it. I had to see this great country where these heroes had come from. I had to go and see America. I discussed it with my parents, but it just seemed to be a pipedream. They could not afford to buy me a ticket to see America. No way.

So I went back to school at age fifteen. My childhood education was not unusual. As many students find, it was often boring, with some exceptions. One of these was my very first day in the first grade in 1942. In those days, there were no kindergartens or nursery schools, so my first day in any school was the first day in the first grade. I remember Moe bringing me to school and trying to assure me that all would be okay. I was nervous because I had never been in such an environment with so many children and with an adult watching over us who was not my mother or father.

But as I came home at the end of that first day, I vividly recall being quite excited because I had learned the letter *O*. Six years old, and all I had learned thus far was the letter *O*. We worked hard in school and did a lot of homework in the evening, studying from seven to eleven o'clock almost every evening, Monday through Friday. School hours were from nine to twelve and from one to four. We had Wednesday afternoons off, but we also went to school Saturday mornings from nine until twelve. Since there are so many tongues spoken throughout Europe, schoolchildren learn to speak, read, and write another language very early in life. We studied Dutch, French, and English in the sixth grade.

I would walk home for lunch at noon. It was about eight blocks away. Moe would always serve us lunch, of course, but one day I came home, and Pa was there. He told us, "Moe is in the hospital," and as he stood at the table with bread and knife in hand, he said, "All right, boys. Tell me once how many slices of bread you want because I am slicing only once and that's it." What a shock this was to me. First of all, Moe was not there, and Moe did not talk like that. Pa was always at work during lunch. When Moe was there, there was a gentle, loving atmosphere that allowed us to ask for an extra slice of bread if we were hungry. But that day was different.

Not that Pa was mean. He was a wonderful, gentle man and loving father. But Moe not being there made a lasting impression on me that I still remember to this day. There was an empty feeling. It shows that there was a motherly love at lunchtime that I had always taken for granted. It made me think: *Is this what life would be like if Moe were never to return?* I did not like that thought at all. I went back to school feeling that something was painfully missing. I think this incident proved how deep my love for my mother was, and I had not realized it before then.

Well, was I glad to see Moe home again a few days later from the hospital. Pa fulfilled a different role. He was the leader, a stable rock we could count on. I had a very good relationship with Pa. I remember him telling me that when you are Christians, as we were, it's like being a prince in God's kingdom. We are royalty in God's domain. I had a hard time understanding the comparison when I was a child, but it certainly was a comforting thought.

Aunt Jen, Moe's sister, was very good to us. She would often bring a gift for us when she came over. She never married, and not far from where Pa worked and where I went to the *First Christelijke Hogere Burgerschool*, she was an administrative nurse in a large hospital/nursing home. Sometimes I would visit her. I have very fond memories of how pleasant and kind she was. Moe had two brothers, Uncle Jan and Uncle Henk, as well as two sisters, Aunt Jen and Aunt Bets. All were wonderful relatives we always enjoyed visiting.

After the war, during the lunch hour, the milkman would usually come to the door. He came every day because, in those days, no one had a refrigerator. I always looked forward to seeing him. He had a horse-drawn milk wagon. He let me pat the horse sometimes. He was nice to me but was always businesslike. I wanted to be his friend, but he seemed to be too busy to make friends with anyone. One day, though, as I lingered around his wagon, waiting for him to come out of our apartment, I got up the nerve to ask him if I could ride with him sometime. Well, to my great surprise, he said, "Do you want to go with me now?" I did not know what that would entail. For how long and how far would we ride? But it was too attractive an offer to pass up, so I said yes.

Well, he got me up on the high seat, sat next to me, and said something like, "Gitty-up." Then the horse started walking. *What a view!* I thought, looking down at the horse and at the people around me. I was so excited to see the world from so high above the city street level. Then he lifted the reigns up and down, said something else, and the horse started trotting. What a great sensation that was for this ten-year-old. The sound of the horse's hooves clopping on the cobblestones was just cool. But when he went around the corner at a full gallop, while the wind was blowing in my face, I had to hold on.

We went to the Willebrordersplein and down another street, made a few stops, and when he came to a stop at his next customer's house, I knew I had to get off and get to school. I was late, and I had disappointed the teacher and later my parents for having gone with the milkman. I was never to do that again.

The other person to make a daily delivery to our house was Mr. Schutte from Ulrich Bakery, which was located on the Straatweg. On the bakery wall was a big sign that said, "*Sterker en groot, door Ulrich's brood*" which means, "Stronger and big, because of Ulrich's bread." Mr. Schutte was a very nice man. His bakery cart always smelled so good, the smell of fresh bread. When food was still scarce after the war, Mr. Schutte was occasionally able to sell or give us a little extra bread because, as he would say, "You have a whole family to feed, so here is some extra."

He mentioned to Moe that his wife and he had not had any milk for a long time. So on a few Saturdays, Rien or Joop and I went to his house. We walked down the Bergweg, made a left on the Zwart Jansstraat, and a right on the Burgemeester Roos Straat, third house on the left, and delivered a small bottle of milk and two eggs to them. They were very grateful for the gesture. Their faces lit up at the sight. Milk and eggs were still rare delicacies even a few months after the war.

MRS. BROWN

Mrs. Brown (*Mevrouw Bruin*) lived upstairs on the fourth floor. She had moved in right after the war. She played a big part in our lives.

There was no separate entrance to her apartment. She and any visitors would come up the thirty-two steps to our apartment, through our hallway, and then up to her apartment. She was elderly, dressed in black clothes all the time, and frequently told us that she was very frail, weak, sickly, and needed a lot of help.

Moe took the brunt of all this. Because she was so good-natured, she was always ready to help Mrs. Brown. And help her Moe did. Mrs. Brown, we think, really took advantage of Moe. Moe would go up in the morning and help her get dressed, put her hose on, and do other things for her. She'd go up in the evening and take Mrs. Brown's hose off and help her again. Mrs. Brown would often say, "Oh, my heart." Sometimes she would bang on the floor with her cane for Moe to come upstairs. This went on for years.

One day, after Dr. Du Puis had visited Mrs. Brown, Moe asked the doctor on his way out, "Doctor, how is Mrs. Brown's heart?"

"Her heart? She has a strong heart like a young person!" he answered. Moe was shocked and could hardly believe it. Moe was never paid for her services, but Mrs. Brown would sometimes give us something for our birthdays. Queen Juliana became the new queen in 1948, replacing Queen Wilhemina. New pennies were issued with Juliana's image on them, and Mrs. Brown gave Jack three of those new pennies for his birthday, along with ten guilders, which was very nice.

Heertje, Mrs. Brown's nephew, would come to visit her once in a while, as did Kippetje (small chicken). Kippetje was a nickname we had given her. Her real name was Coba Kelders. She was small and had a very high-pitched voice. She was an old maid from church, and she was very nice and friendly.

One of my favorite teachers was Miss van Meeuwen. She was my teacher in the fourth and fifth grade. I got along very well with her and performed well. The school I attended was called the Juliana van Stolberg School. It was not a public school but a Dutch Reformed church school. I went there from September 1942 until July 31, 1949.

My report card says that I had finished the sixth grade with a great satisfaction record and a very good behavioral record.

Next, I went first to the *First Christelijke Hogere Burgerschool* on the Henegouwerplein in Rotterdam. I completed the first year in 1950 with an average grade of 6.27, satisfactory (four was failing). In that school, I had a history teacher who was just excellent. He would sit in the front of the class; teach a lesson; check that we had done our homework; and if everything seemed in order, he would tell a fascinating story from history that was not in the textbooks. Now, if only one person in the class misbehaved or had not done his or her homework, there would be no bonus story during the last ten minutes of the class. Very soon, everyone realized what a treat his stories were, so no one wanted to be guilty of ruining the bonus story.

He told us the story of a German prince in the Middle Ages who visited a neighboring area. The king of that area did not like the prince. He was a former enemy. He invited the prince to take a bath in his newly installed facility. While the young monarch was leisurely bathing, he suddenly realized that he could not turn the water off and could not open the door to get out of the bathing chamber.

As the water level got higher and higher, the prince started dog paddling because he didn't know how to swim. As the water kept rising, since there was no handle for him to grab, he became conscious of the fact that he might drown in this regal bathhouse. What a situation to be in! Then suddenly, above the bath area, the king appeared. He started speaking to the prince, letting him know that the prince's life was now in his hands. As his victim struggled to stay alive, the king said he could either drain the water or let the prince drown.

Relishing his position of power, the king recalled the prince's past mishaps and said, "Those are never to occur again." Yet all the while, the king struggled with his conscience. *Should I just let the prince drown or let him live?* While the prince begged for his life, the king was very tempted to let the prince drown. Finally, after our teacher had kept us in suspense, he told us that the king had mustered up some compassion and decided to drain the water and let the prince out of his misery. That was a relief.

Another time, he explained how a person was knighted. He got one student to play the role of the king and another to play the role of the vassal. The king stood up front, and the vassal to be knighted kneeled in front of the king. Then the teacher would give the king the words to say, would have him raise a fake sword that was then placed on one shoulder and then the other, thus proclaiming the vassal into knighthood. He explained what it all meant in those days.

He would bring such amazing stories and illustrations that, without any discipline problems, he kept us in the palm of his hand. I always looked forward to his class. And he just sat there as I don't remember seeing him even standing. He had perfect control of his class. Everyone was very careful to not be the cause of any mishap that would disrupt the class. We respected him and we loved him, and as we did, he rewarded us with the bonus stories.

The *First Christelijke Hogere Burgerschool* was a preparatory school for college, although only wealthy people in Holland ever went to college; and we were certainly not in that category at all. It was really just middle school for me, and maybe I would be able, hopefully, to go to some high school later on.

I finished the first year of this middle school and had started the second year when Moe became very ill. She had developed breast cancer and other problems and was hospitalized more than once. We were not privileged to know the details. Those things were just not talked about. It was just, "Moe is sick. She had to see the doctors and had to go to the hospital and be operated on."

In the European culture, one just did not talk about personal things readily, such as sex or illnesses. She previously had a miscarriage from which, we later found out, she did not recover quickly. It hurt her emotionally. This time, an abdominal tumor was removed, and later she underwent a bilateral mastectomy. This was undoubtedly a devastating ordeal to have to go through. Pa and Moe were drained financially.

One day, two church elders came to visit Pa and Moe. They came to discuss the "loan." The church taught that the parishioners were not to obtain health insurance but to trust God. Pa had called on the minister for help because he could not afford the hospital bills. The minister "gave" Pa the money to pay the bill. Well, the minister had died, and the elders had come to say it was not a gift—it was a loan. Pa tried to explain, but they insisted that Pa and Moe, over time, pay the whole bill. Well, they did.

The minister, incidentally, was a well-known man in the community. He was involved in politics, had started a political party, and had become a member of Congress (the Dutch Parliament). During the last year of the war, however, Pa learned that the minister had become pro-Nazi while he was a captain in the Dutch Army (a chaplain). This was quite a shock! One day, something embarrassing happened to him. While moving from his house on the Boezemsingel to another house on the Westersingel, the moving truck had an accident. It turned over, and piles of food, very good food, spilled all over the street. This was during the hunger winter when many people were literally starving, including the members of his church. The parishioners never understood this. It was extremely disappointing. I still have an old Dutch Bible that I obtained from Pa and Moe. It was given to them by the church and has the minister's signature in it. Despite the erring shepherd, God was present in that church and used people to get the kingdom's work done.

After Moe recovered, she decided that she wanted to go to work to help the family recover financially. Pa learned of an opportunity for her to operate a bakery store in Delft, but she was not licensed to do that. In Holland, it seems that you have to be licensed for everything you may want to do. Well, in order to run a bakery store, Moe had to take two courses. One was so she could learn the whole process of bread making; and the other, a course in selling bread, was so she could learn the contents of different breads.

She passed both courses and was licensed to operate a bakery store. We were really proud of her for doing that. So we moved to Delft, lived behind the store, and Moe started selling. It was a challenge for all of us, and we all got involved. Pa still worked in Rotterdam and commuted daily. He supervised whenever he could. Moe did the daily ordering of the bread, cookies, pastries, etc. They would be delivered each morning.

Sometimes we ran out by two o'clock or so, and I was sent to the bakery to pick up more bread products on my bicycle. One Saturday afternoon, Jack and I were sent out to pick up three big boxes of Tom Poeses (éclairs). I had one box under my right arm, holding the bike's handlebar with my left hand, while Jack had one box under each arm on the little back seat of the bike. These Tom Poeses had a crusty top and bottom, but the middle was soft custard, so the boxes had to be kept perfectly still and horizontal. The boxes' widths were just long enough for our outstretched arms and hands to hold them.

On Saturday afternoon in Delft, the streets were packed with people, and it was hard to get through traffic. Next to each canal in Delft is a street on either side flanked by row houses. At the edge of the canal were trees—about three feet from the edge of the canal. (See photo.)

Where Jack and John rode their bike, close to the water's edge, outside the trees, with two pastry boxes hanging over the water.

It was difficult to get through the traffic while maintaining a little speed so that I could balance the bicycle. At one point, I said to Jack, "Hold on. Let's go outside the trees. Okay with you?" and he agreed. So we rode outside the trees on the very edge, just next to the water down below. That way we could bypass a lot of traffic.

Jack's left hand, on the outside of the boxes, with Tom's Poeses in them, was probably just about three inches away from the trees. If his hand had just touched any of those trees ever so slightly, we both would have been thrown clear into the canal six to ten feet below, with all the pastries. It was a risk I never took again. I guess we were pretty agile on those bikes. I hate to think what could have happened. Of course, we didn't tell Pa and Moe until much later.

I remember that during my teenage years, there were some interesting stores in our neighborhood in Rotterdam. For one, there was a bakery on Benthuizer Straat named "The Korenaar," which had excellent breads. The aroma of the freshly baked bread from the Korenaar's is something I have not experienced in any other bakery. Then there was "C. Jamin," the chocolate store, with great chocolate delicacies. The name was pronounced "Sjamin," as one word.

On our birthdays, Moe would always do something special. Birthdays had become very important to us because of the war. During the war, especially toward the end, there was always the thought that it might be the last birthday. I would get a "*muirtje*," also called "*muirtaartje*," and some fresh strawberries with real whipped cream. A "*muirtje*," which means a small wall, was made up of ladyfingers soaked in a coffee mixture with some other goodies added, with chocolate jimmies sprinkled on top. We treasured that as a really special treat. It was a cold delicacy Moe built up into a square block that could be sliced and served. It was really delicious. For their birthdays, Pa would always get gladiolas from Moe, and Moe would get tulips from Pa. (What else in Holland, right?)

Other delicacies from local bakeries, such as the Korenaar or van Wandelen and others were *Marsepein* (a pastry with petit fours), almond bread baked with sugar and fine ground almonds, *Bokkepootjes*, which means small goatlegs because the middle of the éclair-size pastry was white and the ends had been dipped in chocolate.

Then there were *Boterletters*, which were flat, circular cakes made with almond bread in the middle, baked with butter, crusty on the outside—an excellent pastry. When Christmas came, all the above were served as usual; and in our Christmas stocking, we would also get a chocolate letter in the shape of our first name initial, so I would always get a *J* for Jan (my Dutch name, pronounced "Yahn"). It was made up of solid, hard, dark chocolate about six inches high, and we would take a few days to eat this, piece by piece. None of these were available during the war, of course.

Once we were settled in Delft, I began school, at age 14, at the *Christelijke Lyceum* during the second half of the year. The change was very difficult for me. First, I wanted to go to America. Second, I wanted to help Pa and Moe by making money for the family. My math teacher did not give me a good grade. I don't think he gave any of us a good grade. He could not keep order. He invited trouble with his behavior. The chairs in the class were not nailed to the ground. They were the kind that had small writing desks attached on the left side, in front, almost like an arm support, but you could put books and papers on it. So the chairs were movable.

One time a student in the back row put his back against the wall and pushed all the chairs in front of him forward about six to ten inches. This produced some noise, of course. The teacher, who was writing on the blackboard when this happened, turned around looking very furious. He got red in the face and said, "Who did that?" Well, naturally, no one owned up to it. He asked it again—no response. Well, it got so bad he walked out of the classroom and went to the principal. He threatened to seriously reprimand us. Some kid in the front row went forward and locked the door. The teacher came back with the principal, could not get in, knocked on the door, and we heard, "Open this door now!" What a mess. This teacher managed to bring the worst out of us, while the other history teacher in Rotterdam got the best out of us. What a difference.

I had a bad time in that school and was not well motivated. My mind was elsewhere all the time. Having attended about half a year from 1950–1951, my grades were 5.62 average and 5.69. Six was passing, so I did not get promoted. The note on my report card said, "General impression of John: weak and not enough effort. He must try a lot harder." The 1951–52 year went better: 6.15 average grade. I did not set the world on fire, but I did improve.

In Delft, Pa and Moe started the bakery store business that had been previously owned by Mr. van Wingerden, who lived upstairs in the front room. He owned the building as well. He had a reputation of being somewhat tightfisted. He once had an employee who baked cookies for him. It was the employee's last day, and just before he left, Mr. van Wingerden said to him, "Would you like to take a couple of cookies home with you?"

"Yes," the boy replied.

"That will be two cents," Mr. van Wingerden said.

His tightness with money showed up later when we began noticing that Mr. van Wingerden would slip out of his room at night when all of us were in bed, go downstairs very quietly, and take a couple of cookies from any of the tin cookie boxes in the store. This went on for quite a while. Moe felt sort of sorry for him and just did not say anything. If he had asked for two cookies a day, Pa and Moe would have given them to him.

One day, Martin was home from the navy for the weekend, and we discussed the cookie-stealing situation. Martin thought it would be a good idea to pile up some empty tin cookie containers at the inside entrance of the store so that if someone in the dark would just touch one of them, all the tin cans would fall over and make a terrible racket on the white, stone floor. The floor had beautifully designed tiles but no rugs or carpet. That way, it was easy to clean, looked very attractive, and was quite durable.

So that evening, around 10:30 p.m., Martin strategically piled up the empty cans. Well, all the lights were turned off, and at about 11:15 p.m. Pa and Moe had been talking in the living room located behind the store when they decided to have a cup of tea. Moe went to the kitchen, and Pa went to the store to get something to have with the tea. He completely forgot about the tin cans and promptly walked right in to them, making a terrible, explosion-like noise, waking everybody up.

Mr. van Wingerden hurried downstairs, wondering what in the world happened. Pa explained that some cans fell over and apologized. It was a terrible commotion, but we all had a big laugh about how this great idea by Martin, had backfired. I do believe that the cookie stealing diminished after that incident, though.

During my second year at the *Lyceum* (middle school), at age fifteen, I volunteered to leave school and go to work to help make money for the family. I did not mind this at all because I wanted to see America. Pa kept telling me that I still needed to get a good education so I could get a good job in the future. I had my eyes on America, not on obtaining any good job in Holland for the future. So I worked on a farm outside Delft as a farm worker, picking tomatoes, cutting kale, digging up potatoes, and doing other chores.

Later, we moved back to Rotterdam because Moe had developed arthritis from standing on the stone floor most of the day. Once we were in an apartment in Schiebroek, a suburb of Rotterdam, the arthritis healed up. I worked as a clerk at a tin plate factory and then as a clerk for the Cohen Wine distillery. Another job I had was as a driver for a furrier store on the *Lijnbaan*, the major shopping area in the heart of Rotterdam. I really enjoyed riding around on that three-wheeler. Above the two front wheels, there was a large, rectangular, wooden box for the cardboard boxes with fur coats; and the back part was basically a motorcycle. All I could personally afford was a bicycle, so riding a motorcycle was pretty exciting. I recall that on one rainy day, as I was riding that three-wheeler, the traffic came to an abrupt halt, and I was going too fast to stop in time. I was about to crash, hard, into the car in front of me. The wet cobblestone roadway was very slippery, the box in front of me was heavy, and the back part where I was sitting was light. So, when I applied the brakes, nothing happened. I was sliding straight for the car in front of me, and there was nothing I could do about it. I quickly imagined the box with furs blowing open, the lid flying off, and fur coats strewn across the road for all to see. Just as I was about to hit the back of the car, it pulled forward fast enough so that I did not touch his bumper at all, a very close call. I thanked God for rescuing me from a potentially embarrassing, if not dangerous, situation that could have cost me the job as well—a very close call indeed.

HOW TO GET TO AMERICA?

I had to see America somehow. I applied to the Merchant Marine Academy to become a Merchant Marine Officer; but I did not qualify because I did not have enough schooling. I tried to get a job with the airlines. I was turned down as well. Finally (I was now seventeen), I applied to the training school for sailors with the Holland America Line. I was accepted there and completed the three-week course and then applied for a job on one of the ocean-going vessels, which happened to be the biggest one in Holland: the *Nieuw Amsterdam* or *New Amsterdam*. She was thirty-three thousand tons—just huge. I was hired as a kettle boy, which was the lowest rank of all the 1100 crew members; but I didn't care. I was going to see America.

On the big day of departure, I was dressed in a suit and tie. I was wearing an overcoat as well—to make a decent impression on my new boss, I suppose. As I was boarding the ship, I went up the gangplank, where everyone else went, or so I thought. But I was with the passengers. The first person I saw was one of the pursers who greeted passengers. He said, "Good morning, sir." I introduced myself. He asked for my cabin papers, which, of course, I did not have. I told him I was the new kettle boy.

He was not very excited. In fact, he was rather stunned and could not believe what I was saying. I was too well dressed for a kettle boy. Finally, I convinced him that I was a new crewmember by showing him my crewmember booklet. His surprised look changed to the very serious demeanor of one trying to be more intimidating. "You don't belong here, boy. Get down below."

"Yes, sir," I replied accommodatingly and marched off down below.

I asked for the boatsman, who was my new boss, but he was busy on deck. Someone else showed me where my cabin was, which I shared with three other sailors. I put my bag down and went upstairs on deck to watch us leave the Rotterdam harbor. And watch I did. I saw all the sailors very busy with the heavy ropes, talking loudly, with frequent curse words. It was a thrilling sight to see this huge ship slowly moving away from the dock.

I spotted my parents and Jack on the pier. Waving to them, with this separation and an uncertain future, I felt overwhelmed with sad emotions. Realizing that I was really going across the ocean, I had a little bit of a sinking feeling and I thought, *You know, these things sink sometimes. Remember the Titanic?*

The *New Amsterdam* glided majestically down the Maas River toward Hoek of Holland where the ships leave the mainland and enter the North Sea on their way to the Atlantic Ocean. I noticed then that it had become quite windy.

I must have been daydreaming, trying to take it all in that I was finally, really going to America, because I was startled when a man walked up to me and said suddenly, "Are you Jan van den Berge?"

"Yes, sir," I answered, standing at attention.

"You are the new kettle boy? There is work for you to do downstairs. Why are you standing here?" I got the message. My job was to keep the sailors' rooms and the mess hall/dining room clean, to make up the sailors' bunks and serve the meals, to clean the dishes, etc. You see, kettle boy was four ranks below that of "sailor." I slept in the most forward and lowest cabin of the ship, just near the anchor. I would soon find out that when the ship goes up and down on the ocean, that area of the ship moves the most.

As they usually did each night, the sailors, having worked hard on deck when the ship left port, gathered at the crewmembers' bar for a few beers before dinner. One of the older sailors spotted me and said, "So, you are new around here?" We had a short conversation as we tried to size each other up. "Here. Have a beer."

I accepted the offer, and as I was about to take a sip, an invisible force opened my hand, and the glass fell to the ground in a thousand pieces. I have no other way to explain this. In the last fifty-five years, I have never dropped another glass since that moment. How embarrassing! I apologized all over the place and helped to clean it up. *What a great start,* I thought. The older sailor did not offer me another glass, and I just walked away, still apologizing. By the way, what was this "invisible" force? Did God just save me from alcoholism? Perhaps he did. I know I have not had a beer since that day.

The work was not very difficult, and I got along pretty well with the men, making friends as I went along, even though I did not fit in so well; I didn't curse, swear, or drink beer.

The wind picked up some more, the ship started moving, and by the time we had gone through the English Channel and entered the Atlantic Ocean, a real storm manifested. All of a sudden, it was as though we were climbing hills. The nose of the ship went up and fell down into the next wave. All loose items had to be stabilized. When the ship went down, you could easily run up the steps by three or four steps at a time. But when the nose came up, it was really hard to climb each individual step. It seemed so heavy. It was not long before I was experiencing a serious case of seasickness.

Everything came up. I carried a paper bag with me at all times and tried to stay in bed as much as I could. But in spite of the sickness, I did not care. I would get to see America. All the portholes were closed, even for the passengers. I did not get to see the ocean much at all.

As a rookie, I had to endure a few things. One day, an old sailor told me that I was to go to the engine room and get the compass key and take it to the bridge so the first mate or the captain could adjust the compass. The explanation was that with the bad weather, the compass could be thrown off a little bit and needed to be adjusted. The engine room was way downstairs in the middle of the ship. The bridge was the highest level upstairs, where the officers who commanded the ship stood and the most experienced sailors were at the wheel, steering the ship. I said, "Yes, sir," and off I went. But something sounded a bit fishy to me.

Even though I had attended the sailors' training school for only three weeks, I had never heard of a compass needing to be adjusted during a voyage in the middle of the ocean. It was done in the harbor. Then I realized they were going to have me carry a very heavy metal adjusting device, such as a big crowbar, and take it about eight or ten levels up to the bridge and then take it down again. It just did not make any sense. So I stayed away for about forty-five minutes, went back, and told the old sailor that the first mate (the first officer just under the captain) wanted to see him. I told him that the officer asked who had sent me and that I told him that he, the sailor, had sent me. That was the end of that incident.

On another occasion, someone sent me to the bridge to get the mail. I was told that once during the trip across the ocean, a mail plane flies over and drops mailbags with mail from home. I had never heard of such a thing, so I went upstairs, walked around for about half an hour, and came back and never said anything to anyone about it. No one asked either. They sort of left me alone after that as far as practical jokes were concerned. I tried to fit in as well as I could, but it was hard because, as I said before, I did not curse and swear, which they did a lot of, and I did not drink beer.

With all the seasickness, it seemed that the trip would never end, but after eight days, the movement of the ship lessened and we sailed smoothly. Everyone was getting excited as we were coming "home" to America. And there it was, suddenly: America on the horizon. We sailed past Long Island on the right, and then, to my left, I suddenly noticed the Statue of Liberty. What an impressive sight. I had heard so much about it, and to actually see it majestically greeting guests of America, representing the country that goes around the world, setting people free from tyrants—what a moment. Finally, I was in America.

Soon, some American tugboats came to the ship, and we docked in Hoboken, New Jersey. These tugboats were different from the Dutch tugboats. They seemed more powerful somehow. After the passengers had gone ashore, the crew had eaten, and I had done my cleaning chores, I went on deck and was able to see the first real Americans on American soil. I was really looking forward to talking with them. I had learned some English in school, and I wanted to test my language skills right away. I walked up to a longshoreman and said something like, "Good morning. How are you, sir?"

Well, what I got back was anything but the Pall Mall British I had learned in Holland. It was a combination of some slang and rough, very masculine verbalism I had never heard before. I didn't understand a word he said. Of course, every third word was a curse word of some sort. I was very disappointed. First, I thought that my teacher had let me down; but later I learned differently.

Once I went ashore, I found out there were three ways by public transportation to go to Manhattan (where I wanted to see Times Square and Forty-second Street): by ferry, bus, or subway. Each day, I did some exploring and used a different route and a different mode of transportation. One day, while on Forty-second Street, I got hungry and went into a deli where a lot of people were buying and eating all sorts of sandwiches and drinking coffee, juice, and whatever else was available.

I followed the crowd and took a number like everyone else; but when I got to the counter, I was stuck. The man said, "What do you want?" in a loud and harsh voice. I didn't know. I looked past his head at the menu, which was plastered all across the wall behind him. It listed many items, none of which were familiar to me. But then I spotted *eggs*. So I asked him for "de-viled eggs," with emphasis on the *viled*. "Oh! You want deviled eggs." He straightened me out nicely.

Once I got started with the Holland America Line (HAL) the first trips were on the *New Amsterdam*, from July 14, 1953–November 3, 1953. On the fifth trip across the ocean to New York and back, I was promoted to light sailor. Subsequently, I signed on with the *Aalsdijk*, a HAL freighter, where I sailed for five ocean-going voyages to various US harbors, such as Galveston; Houston; Corpus Christi; Boston; Philadelphia; Baltimore; and, of course, New York City until July 1954.

John and a co-sailor aboard Holland America's *Aalsdijk*

Then I was promoted to sailor under the wages (one rank below full sailor) when I went on the *Maasdam*, another HAL passenger ship. On the sixth trip, while onboard the *Maasdam*, I finally made it to full sailor. I was on the *Maasdam* from September 1954 to April 1955. Next, I was on the *Westerdam*, a combination freight and passenger ship, as a sailor for four voyages until August 1955.

Life on these ships was exciting at times but also boring. It sounds pretty romantic for a young man to go see the world, to see all those different cities. After awhile, though, with very few exceptions, all the harbor towns looked alike to me.

I remember being in Havana before Castro was in power. I was there in August 1953, and it was very hot. The *New Amsterdam* was at anchor in the small Havana harbor. We were allowed to go ashore and walk around all over the place. A couple of times, a young, attractive girl would walk along and invite my friend and me to come to her house. It was very clear that the poor thing was a prostitute, and we declined. There were X-rated movie theaters, lots of bars—Cuban music blaring from most of them—and lots of poor people around. Finally, we got pretty tired, and my friend and I decided to sit at one of the outdoor cafes and get something to drink. "What do we drink?" we asked.

The most popular drink in Havana was, and probably still is, rum and coke, which is what one man sitting next to us recommended. He sounded perfectly fine, and thus we had rum and coke. After a while, the man got up; and we noticed that as he got out of the café, he was wobbling badly as if he had had a lot to drink. I thought that that was strange because I had the same drink he had and it did not affect me at all. Well, it was time to go, and as soon as I got up, it hit me too. Rum and coke does not affect you until you start walking. I wobbled too—all the way to the ship. The next morning I woke up with my first (and last) hangover.

When the *New Amsterdam* wanted to leave the next day, it found that its anchor chains had been twisted. The ship had pivoted around its two anchor cables with the high and low tides. So some tugboats were called in, and they spent more than a half day untangling the heavy anchor cables.

The passenger ships, the *Maasdam* and the *New Amsterdam*, cruised into the Caribbean. That was a lot of fun for sailors and tourists alike. A ship full of people wanting to relax and have fun in the beautiful, warm climate with light blue waters, through which one could see the propellers of the ship, was pretty cool stuff. We helped the passengers get ashore in ports like St. Thomas, Aruba, and others.

Where the big ships could not dock, we did this with the ship's ferryboats, which were lowered from outside the promenade deck. They were like big lifeboats with a small motor. We enjoyed riding in those.

Yet, I still had not found a way to stay in America, which is what I really wanted to do. There were things about America that I loved wherever I went. I really enjoyed visiting Galveston and Houston, as well as Corpus Christi. Of course, I loved New York City. I never got to know Baltimore, Philadelphia, or Boston very well then because during the three days visiting those cities, I was allowed ashore only in the evening.

On the ships, experiences went from one extreme to another. One freighter took us to Halifax, Nova Scotia, in the winter. That was extremely cold. The weather had been rough, and water had sprayed all over the ship. When we sailed into Halifax harbor, six inches of ice had coated the deck, railings, and anchors. Thick ice was everywhere. The decks were extremely slippery. We managed somehow. On the other extreme, it was very hot in Havana; and the summers in New York City were sometimes unbelievably humid.

There was one evening in New York City when it was too hot to stay in the cabin on the freighter at bedtime. The ship was made of steel and had no air-conditioning, there was no breeze outside, and the humidity was unbearable, so I decided to take a very light blanket and sleep on the deck, thinking it might cool off a little during the night. Well, during my sleep, a giant New York City mosquito must have bitten my lower lip because I woke up with my lip being five or six times its normal size. What a shock! It took a few days for it to go down.

The other extreme weather is the storms on the ocean. On the *Aalsdijk*, we had picked up freight in Hamburg, Germany, and had set off for Rotterdam, normally less than a day's journey. Unexpectedly, a storm came up that wouldn't quit. There were very high waves on the North Sea, and those waves are shorter than the Atlantic Ocean waves, which made our voyage very dangerous. The ship was lifted by one high wave and then plunged down deep into the next wave. It then vibrated and shook, especially at the very front and at the very back part, also called the "poop deck." Our cabins were under the "poop deck," which meant that we felt the effects of every single wave we crossed.

I remember one time, when I had managed to fall asleep, I woke up because of a tremendous jolt. I looked up and saw my roommate in the top bunk just across from me horizontally bouncing up and down in his bed about two to three feet high, and of course, I was doing the same thing. Sometimes the nose of the ship plunged so deeply into the next wave that the propellers in the rear of the ship came out of the water, which, as you could imagine, caused tremendous vibrations. This was one of those occasions. At that particular moment, yours truly was reciting a few selected prayers. The whole ship was bending lengthwise like a slackened seesaw.

On the deck, we had strung ropes between the "poop deck" and the main, middle section of the ship, the midships, so one could hold on while trying to walk to and from midships (where we ate three meals a day). Only the most experienced sailors were allowed to steer the ship to keep her nose straight into the wind and waves, because if the ship were to go sideways, it would likely be overwhelmed by the high waves and go down. It took three days to finally get into Rotterdam harbor.

CHAPTER 9

ONE WAY TO NEW YORK CITY

In late 1955, I received notice that the Royal Dutch Air Force needed my services. They just could not live without me, apparently. I was drafted for a two-year stint unless I wanted to serve longer. I left the Holland America Line and was sent to Nijmegen for boot camp training as a private. Nijmegen was the area where a great battle had been fought during World War II, which was depicted in the movie, "A Bridge Too Far."

I became a corporal and then a drill sergeant instructor. It was not a bad life—sometimes easy, sometimes not. In particular, I recall one of those times when life was not made easy for any of us. On that occasion, we were camped out in the woods somewhere next to a lake far away from home base. We were to defend ourselves in case of enemy attack. Another platoon was to attack us sometime in the near future. Well, we figured that the lake was a natural barrier that should be easy to defend because the enemy was not likely to cross the water without being seen. So we set up camp on the one side of the lake. We dug manholes, the whole works. As time went by, it got a little colder, but still we waited patiently, and we were going to be there for at least three weeks.

John in the Royal Dutch Air Force (1955)

While we waited for our enemy attack, the weather turned for the worst, and the lake began to freeze over. We were still outdoors in our manholes, ready to defend ourselves at a moment's notice. However, we did have suitable sleeping bags, which helped a lot. We were always camouflaged, our faces painted black, rifles ready at all times. Weeks ahead of time, we had been trained for this sort of thing. The waiting, however, seemed to be the biggest enemy for me.

Ultimately, the enemy never showed up. So, disgruntled and worn out, we packed up and went home to the base. We marched for miles with our full backpacks and rifles. We were tired. I was dragging my feet, as everyone else was. I think we suffered from "battle fatigue," although we hadn't fought anything or anyone. We stopped on the way at a little food place, some sort of restaurant/gas station where we could use the bathroom. As I began to wash my hands, I looked in the mirror and thought, *Who is that man behind me?* There wasn't anyone there as I looked around. Then I realized I was seeing myself in the mirror. I did not recognize the man looking back at me. I was so dirty, painted, and perfectly disguised under a coat of grimy sweat. *No wonder the enemy could not find us!* I mused, still staring at my reflection in disbelief.

Back on the road, as we were marching, wondering how far we had yet to walk before we would reach our base, we noticed some military people standing around up ahead. As we got closer, they got into formation, facing away from us. Upon reaching them, they started to play music. This was the Royal Dutch Air Force Marching Band.

Lieutenant Schelberg, our commander, had arranged for the band to meet us for the last mile or so before getting home. They played John Philip Sousa marches, and how those picked us up. All of a sudden, I was not tired anymore. I have never again experienced the positive effect of music as I did on that occasion. It really touched our hearts—at least it did mine. It was very uplifting for all of us, and we were quite grateful to the lieutenant for arranging such an escort for the platoon.

I spent most of my time in Nijmegen except for the last part of my tour of duty, when I was stationed at a camp named Woensdrecht Air Base in the South of Holland, out in no-man's land. On weekends, I took up airplane gliding. After a number of weekend lessons, I managed to get a solo pilot's certificate and did thirteen solo flights. That was pretty exciting and exhilarating, to be up in the air, flying around like a bird, without any noise from engines—just the wind and the beauty of nature up there.

A very interesting incident occurred while I was based at Woensdrecht. One day, I received a call to come to the main gate. I had a guest. To my great surprise, it was Captain Brackx from America. How in the world did he find me there, and why did he come? I had met Captain Brackx in New York while I was a sailor on one of the freighters of the Holland America Line.

Whenever we were in New York, I would usually visit the Seamen's Institute in Lower Manhattan. It was a place where seamen from a number of different nations would meet with some of their countrymen. There was a Dutch floor, a Norwegian floor, and so on. On one occasion, I was at the Institute on the Dutch floor when my boatsman, Mr. Frank Brackx, was also there. Most of us would play pool or table tennis, but he was there to meet his brother, Captain Brackx, who was an American Merchant Marine sea captain.

The boatsman introduced me to Captain and Mrs. Brackx, a lovely lady, and we talked for a while. I guess they took a liking to me and invited me to go with them that evening to their house on Long Island. Thus, a friendship started, and I would contact them whenever I came to New York. This occurred a couple of times before I had to go into the Air Force in Holland. I really did not know if I would ever see them again.

So you can understand my surprise when he visited me on the air base. *How in the world did he find me and why?* were the questions that repeatedly ran through my mind as I went to meet him at the gate. As we sat in the cafeteria, he explained that he had to deliver a merchant ship from New York to Istanbul. He had taken his Cadillac on the ship and drove from Istanbul through Europe to Holland, where he was going to pick up another ship to captain back to New York. So he decided to look me up. We talked at length, and he finally said, "Vandenberge, you have to come to America."

That was music to my ears. "How can I do that?" I asked. He said he would try to help me find a sponsor and see what else he could do. We had a wonderful visit, and as he left, he wished me well. He suggested that I apply for a visa as soon as possible and went on his way. Well, he certainly helped and arranged for his friend, Captain Martin Ruygrok, to be my sponsor.

To be a sponsor meant that one would be financially responsible for me for five years in case I became a liability to the state where I was residing. He was a retired Merchant Marine Captain; and his office, from which he still did some business, was next door to the immigration office in New York City, so he was familiar with some of the immigration officers.

On my next trip back to Rotterdam, I went to the American Consulate on Captain Brackx's advice, and applied for a visa to immigrate to America. In the meantime, in 1958, after I left the Royal Dutch Air Force, I obtained a job as a cabin steward on the *Nieuw Amsterdam* in June to start sailing again in preparation for possible immigration. This was the same ship I made my first trip on as a kettle boy.

A cabin steward is on duty at night, from ten o'clock to six in the morning, and attends to the needs of the passengers in the evening and during the night. I would serve patrons late-night snacks or drinks when they came back from entertainment upstairs. I served them in any way I could. If passengers placed their shoes outside their cabin door, I would collect them and polish them during the night. I also had a part-time job as an assistant bartender with Mr. Tan, a very nice Chinese gentleman who was the bartender in the first-class bar, from five to about eight o'clock in the evening during the cocktail hours. One day, I served a drink to Mr. Van Heflin, the movie star.

Mr. Tan was a character. One evening, I went to the bar and told him I could not work because I had a very sore throat and felt a bad cold coming on. He said, "Just a minute. I'll fix you up." Well, he mixed me a hot toddy (consisting of some rum and hot lemon juice), and he gave me two aspirins. I drank down that tall glass, and I declare, the pain went away very quickly. I did stay and work without feeling much of anything, actually. I had no effect from the alcohol at all and remained quite steady on my feet. The cold never developed, and the sore throat stayed away as well. A couple of years later, I had a sore throat and a cold like that. So I tried the hot toddy deal, but it did not work. I guess I didn't have Mr. Tan's knack in preparing it.

It was an exciting time working on the ships. Rubbing elbows with all kinds of people from all walks of life was intriguing to me. As a steward, I had direct contact with the passengers, which I did not have as a sailor or a kettle boy. Sometimes I was assigned to operate the elevators, which went from C deck to the promenade deck, where there was almost always some kind of entertainment—usually a band and dancing. As crewmembers, we could not participate in the dancing; but I enjoyed watching people.

I also got to know some of the musicians, and I really enjoyed the music. On one trip, a steward, who was also a vocalist, sang with the band. They sang some very good American songs like Glen Miller's "Chattanooga Choo Choo." We did get to see some movies in one of the theaters.

At times, I served passengers tea and goodies on the promenade deck. That was a lot of fun. Passengers were lounging in the deckchairs in the ocean breeze, and the incredible view of the ocean was just great. It was calming and peaceful. I recall that, earlier, while on lookout duty as a sailor on the very nose of one of the ships during really foggy weather, I was to report seeing any other ships or lights or sounds by phone to the officers on the bridge. Sometimes dolphins would swim just in front of the bow and then jump out of the water and dive back in.

At night, when there was a lot of plankton in the water, I could see the outline of the dolphins, as the plankton lit up when I looked over the railing, straight down below. When they jumped up and were above the water, their outline was not there; only when they were underwater could I see the outline of their graceful, streamlined forms. What a spectacular sight that was.

One time, I was fortunate enough not to be on duty as a lookout on the bow. I was on the *SS Maasdam* in 1956, leaving New York City for Holland when it was very foggy. It was about 8:00 p.m. when I had gone to bed. Suddenly, at about 9:00 p.m., there was a loud thud and a sound like a huge explosion and a rattling that was like a machine gun firing. The ship shook badly, and I had no idea what was happening. I had never experienced anything like that before.

My roommate, an older, experienced sailor, ran into the room, grabbed his life jacket, and ran out. He said, "Get upstairs now!" I wondered if we were sinking. Once upstairs, I saw smoke and fog and, of course, darkness. I just saw the side of another ship, very closeby, drifting backward. It turned out that we had collided with a Swedish freighter. The nose of our ship had actually penetrated the cargo area in the side of the other ship.

The officers had come down to assess the damage and to see if the hull was cut and whether there was a chance we might start sinking. The watertight doors, separating parts of the ship, had been closed. We did not sink, and neither did the other vessel. We did have a large hole in the bow below the waterline, but there was no danger of sinking. Incidentally, the machine gun sounds were caused by metal plates being ripped apart at the time of the collision when the bolts, which kept the plates together, were forcibly torn out. It was a very scary experience. The sailor who stood at lookout on the bow was able to run back just seconds before the ships collided, and he was minimally hurt. In the photos, you can see the big hole in the nose of the ship; and the deck damage was right above where I was sleeping in my cabin. The freighter was empty—incidentally, there was no cargo.

The *Maasdam's* deck damage after colliding with a Swedish freighter

The *Maasdam's* bow damage after colliding with a Swedish freighter

We turned back to New York City and spent close to a month in dry dock in Brooklyn before we could go back to Holland.

Well, back to the *New Amsterdam,* which is the ship I was on again after I had served my duty in the Royal Dutch Air Force from 1956–1958. The photo shows my switch from Air Force Sergeant to steward in 1958.

The ship I was on now, the *Nieuw Amsterdam,* was on a Caribbean cruise schedule, sailing between New York and the Caribbean five times, after which she would return to Rotterdam. At the end of the second cruise, we arrived in Hoboken, New Jersey, in the morning. The passengers were disembarking, and usually there were not many immigration or naturalization activities because we did not come from Europe.

A few agents did come on board; and soon after their arrival I suddenly was called to report to the purser's office. Never having been called there, I really had no idea what the reason behind this call might be. One of the Dutch purser officers directed me to see an immigration and naturalization officer by the name of Mr. Fair. Mr. Fair, a short man with a low, booming voice, said to me, "Are you Jan?"

John as a steward (1958). Note the Empire State Building in background.

"Yes, sir," I replied.

"Where is your passport?" he asked with a tone that implied that I should have had the passport with me right then and there. I told him it was in my cabin.

"Well, go get it!" he said, lifting an eyebrow.

The purser, who had been watching and listening to this little exchange, smiled at me but said nothing. I ran downstairs and started to think that this might be good news in regard to my visa application, but I still wasn't sure. The officer may have had something else in mind. Perhaps he thought I had done something wrong.

When I came back with my passport, Mr. Fair looked at it and took out the little chest X-ray (to make sure I didn't have any T.B., I think), which was part of the process. He looked at it, holding it up to the light, and put it in an envelope. He then stamped the front of my passport in red letters: "Admitted to The United States of America," and said to me, "Jan, you are admitted to America, which means that you can stay here if you want to. Good luck." We shook hands, and he went on his way.

I was stunned. I had waited for this moment since I was nine years old, and now that it was finally happening, I was tongue-tied. But, overcoming my obvious trepidation, I thanked him and started for my cabin. At this moment, the purser, who had been watching me, motioned that I should come with him because someone else wanted to see me. He took me to the chief purser's office, a place where I had never been before, and there were four high-ranking officers waiting for me—and I mean high-ranking because I saw nothing but glistening uniforms with all kinds of stripes and gold and silver curls on their arms.

One of them held my passport in his hand, which had been handed to him by the first purser shortly after we entered the office. To me, this whole situation appeared somewhat threatening. The officer seemed to say, "We have your passport here, and we can keep it if we deem that appropriate."

Then one of the officers asked me what was going on. So I explained that I had applied for a visa a year and half ago and did not know that the request had apparently been granted. He asked what my plans were. I told him that I hoped to be able to immigrate to America someday. Then he asked, "Are you planning to jump ship?"

"No, sir," I replied truthfully. I had not planned to do so. I had not had time to plan anything like that. Things had happened so fast. Well, they warned me that if I were to do anything crazy like that I could be in big trouble with the FBI or other US authorities and I could be arrested. So, for my own good, they said it would be best to stay on the ship and fulfill my obligations to the Holland America Line. They gave the passport back to me with another warning of sorts and let me go.

Once again, I was on my way to my cabin; and as I went, I could still hear Mr. Fair's booming voice resounding, "You have been admitted to the United States of America, and you can stay here if you want to." When I was in my cabin alone, I sat down and thought about what to do. It was obviously up to me. So what options did I have now? I knew from Captain Brackx that the Holland America Line at times was not so nice to their employees.

His brother, Boatsman Brackx, who was my boss on the *Aalsdijk*, had been fired just about one year before his retirement, for no apparent reason at all. He had worked for the company many years and lost his pension along with all his benefits. I had also heard that if the company did not like you, they might make you peel potatoes for the rest of the trip. (I understand that employer-employee relations are much better now. The HAL cruise ships are some of the best in the world—if not the best, as I experienced years later on a delightful cruise with family members.) Well, I had such incredible confidence in what Mr. Fair said and in America, and such little confidence in the officers upstairs with their threats, that the decision came rather easily. I packed everything I had, including my tennis racket with the handle sticking out, into a hand-carried piece of luggage.

My roommates came in at that moment and, of course, asked me what I was doing. So I told them the truth and said that I was leaving to stay ashore. I said good-bye to them and shook their hands as I took in their warnings. They had heard of people doing that and being arrested by the FBI, the Secret Service, the Immigration Service, New York Police, etc. I was told that I was crazy and that they were sure I would be back in handcuffs.

But they did not know Mr. Fair and did not know what he had told me. I realized that there was no sense explaining all of that to them because they would not believe it anyway. I asked them just not to tell anyone that day and walked out, down the hallway, out on the crew's gangplank, and onto the pier. I felt free and relieved; but when I came to the end of the pier, I realized there was a guard who could stop me and ruin everything. Well, I figured I'd just keep walking and perhaps he would not notice me or not bother to interrogate me. I walked past him, looked straight ahead; and when I thought I was getting clear, I heard, "Hey, son. Where are you going?" So I turned around and walked toward him and smiled and said, "Well, I am taking some clothes ashore."

"Oh. I thought you were jumping ship," he said, smiling.

"Ha! Are you kidding?" I said and turned around and just walked away. He never asked any other questions. I knew that the Lord was with me at that point, but I was still nervous.

I quickly went to a phone booth and called Captain Brackx, who happened to be home. "Hello, Captain. Well, I am here, and here to stay," I said, my voice trembling as I pronounced every word. I explained what had occurred, and he sounded very happy that I made it ashore without a hitch.

He said that if they had kept my passport, which he secretly hoped they would have, that he, as an American Merchant Marine Captain, could have prevented that huge ship from leaving the port of New York. He would have been happy to get even with that steamship company because of what they had done to his brother. However, nothing like that happened.

So he suggested that I go to the Seamen's Institute at the foot of Manhattan, get a room there for $1.50 per night, and start looking for a job in New York City. I was most happy to do so. I could not come to see him because he was leaving early in the morning to sail another ship someplace.

I was not afraid of the FBI or any other police because I had total confidence that Mr. Fair knew what he was doing. If I had been afraid of the authorities, I certainly would not have gone to the Seamen's Institute because that would have been a very obvious place for them to look for me, especially on the Dutch floor. Incidentally, little did I realize that this day would be the last day of my merchant marine career, having crossed the ocean fifty-eight times. I slept like a baby that night. I was twenty-two years old.

The next day I started looking for a job. I applied for waiter, dishwasher, handyman, helper on a truck—anything. I looked for three weeks, and the question was always, "Are you a member of a union?" and/or "Are you a US citizen?" Well, of course I wasn't either one. I was getting tired and a bit discouraged, and I was running out of money.

Once in my room, I started to ponder what to do next. I thought of my parents, of course; but they could not help me now, although

I was sure they were praying for me. They did not know what was going on with me, and I had not written them yet after my decision to stay in America. I had told Pa and Moe that when I left the last time I might be able to stay in America.

Normally I wrote my parents regularly; but this time I had to wait till I could tell them something really positive and not what I was experiencing now. Whenever I could, I helped them financially. Usually I brought some gifts for them as well, such as souvenirs and a couple of cartons of Lucky Strike and Camel cigarettes for Pa, who really appreciated that. I missed them, of course, and I was pondering what to do next.

CHAPTER 10

THE START IN BALTIMORE

During one of the ship's crossings, while in the middle of the ocean, I struck up a conversation with a passenger, Linwood Jenkins, who was walking on the promenade deck of the *Nieuw Amsterdam*. He said hello, we talked a little bit as we looked out over the ocean, and I remember he mentioned Billy Graham. He invited me to come and see him sometime if I ever came to Baltimore. He gave me his address and phone number; and just to be polite, I told him that he would be welcome to come and see me in Rotterdam if he wanted to and, in turn, gave him my address. These casual meetings with people happen sometimes on a ship, but I never expected to see him again.

On the next Saturday morning, the ship arrived at 8:00 a.m. in Rotterdam. I left to go ashore at about 9:00 a.m. Even though the crossing takes over a week, I never saw Linwood again during the eight days aboard the ship. It was good to be home again. I spent time with Pa and Moe and Joop, and we talked about a lot of things. There was a lot of news to catch up on since I had last seen them; it had been three weeks.

At about 6:00 p.m., the doorbell rang, and there was Linwood Jenkins. What a surprise. He seemed to be very glad to see me. The reason for his unexpected visit became clear when he explained that he had gone to visit his brother-in-law's parents, an elderly couple, Mr. and Mrs. Visser, who lived in an apartment in Rotterdam.

Mr. and Mrs. Visser did not speak any English except *yes*, *no*, and *coffee*. Linwood had arrived there at 11:00 a.m., and by about 4:00

p.m., although he dearly wanted to do so, he was not able to communicate with the Visser family at all, and he did not know what to do. He had never been in a situation like that before and felt embarrassed and very uncomfortable. Finally, he went through his pockets and found my address.

We had a good time conversing and ate the dinner Moe had prepared for us. We learned that Linwood was going to France and Germany on a tour by himself. If he had gotten so readily stuck in Holland, we wondered how he was going to fare since he was unable to speak the languages of the other countries he intended to visit. So it was decided that Jack would go with him because I had to go back on the ship in three days. In the end, it worked out very well. Jack was able to take time off from work and was happy to accommodate Linwood.

So when I was in New York City and had spent three weeks trying to find a job, unsuccessfully, I decided to call Linwood in Baltimore. He was my last hope because I had no job prospects, was running out of money, and didn't know what else to do. Fortunately, he was home. It was so good to talk with him. He told me to take the Greyhound bus to Baltimore and he'd meet me at the bus station and get me a job.

Linwood met me at the station. Boy, it was good to see him. He took me to his house, where I met his sister, Elizabeth Visser, and her daughter, Ruthie. I was in an American home in this great new country. Everything looked good and smelled good, and my dream was being fulfilled. We ate something. (I was certainly hungry.) Then Linwood and I went out to find me a place to live and helped me rent a room from Mrs. Yingling on Augusta Avenue in Edmondson Village. He lent me $3.00 so that I could pay the $6.00 rent for the first week. When I arrived in Baltimore, I had $3.00 in my pocket. That's all!

That night, again, I slept like a baby. My first day in Baltimore, I had no money; but I was impressed and grateful for friends who were willing to help me get started. I could not wait to get to work in this great country.

The next day, Elizabeth, who worked at a local restaurant named

Champs on the corner of Route 40 and Ingleside Avenue, got me a job as a carhop. My first real job in America!

Linwood asked me on Saturday evening after my arrival if I wanted to go with him the next morning. He said that on Sunday mornings, he usually goes to the local church, Brantly Baptist Church, near Edmondson Village in Baltimore. I agreed because I had a good Christian upbringing in Holland, but in the Merchant Marines there are no churches, so I had not been to any church for a long time.

Linwood, employed at the Western Maryland Railway Company in their freight traffic department, was instrumental in getting Linda Ann Dorn, who also attended Brantly Baptist Church, an interview for a secretarial position in the law department of the same company. Linda, after her sophomore year at Western High School, became a nurse's aid, a "Pinky," and worked during the summer and alternate Saturdays and Sundays while in high school.

She graduated from Western High School in 1955. However, she had decided nursing was not for her, and she went to the Baltimore Business College to become a secretary. Soon after graduation, she was interviewed at the Western Maryland Railway Company and was hired as a secretary for two lawyers in the law department, Mr. Rowland Posey and Mr. Rene J. Gunning.

Thus, Linwood invited me to Brantly Baptist Church. He had told Linda that he had been to Europe, had met a young man from Holland, and that he would bring him to church (although Linwood had not told me about Linda). As it turned out, that was not necessary.

Linwood and I sat in about the fourth row on Sunday, and at age twenty-one, I did not have any trouble spotting this beautiful girl in the choir. I don't remember the sermon for some reason. My head was full of all the new things I was experiencing, including seeing that pretty girl. Well, we were introduced, and, as they say, the rest is history. There was a spark there for both of us.

The next Monday, Linwood asked me, "John, now that you are in this country, what do you want to do, or what do you want to be?" I had no idea. I really didn't. I was just glad to be here. So he said, "Why don't we look through the Yellow Pages?" and we did. We looked alphabetically at accountants, bakers, bankers, and nothing particularly appealed to me until we got to dentists.

"How about becoming a dentist?" I asked.

"Do you want to be a dentist?"

"Yes."

Mind you, I had never thought about being a dentist. It just fell out of my mouth. Linwood called the dental school in Baltimore the next day and made an appointment for me to see the dean of admissions, Dr. Vandenbosche. That was interesting to me, of course, because of the similarity in our names. I later found out that he was originally from Belgium, just south of Holland. I did see him the next day. We greeted each other, and he said, "So you want to be a dentist?"

"Yes, sir. What do I need to do?" Then Dr. Vandenbosche proceeded to review my education, which did not take long. He asked a couple of questions and basically made a checklist of what I needed to do to become a dentist. First, I needed the equivalency of a high school diploma. Dr. Vandenbosche recommended that I go to the library and study to pass a high school equivalency test. Three weeks later, I took the test and, surprise, surprise, I passed!

Solely based on my limited education, I should not have passed the exam; but I will give a little bit of credit to the Dutch Christian schools. In the sixth grade, I did homework with my friend, Nico van Vliet, almost every evening, Monday through Friday from seven to eleven o'clock. We studied hard and were well disciplined. We studied Dutch, English, and French in the sixth grade. We got German in middle school. But I did not take any courses in physics or chemistry, which hurt me later on in college. I also took a dental aptitude test at the dental school, which I passed after the second try.

Taking Dr. Vandenbosche's advice, I took the necessary courses for the freshman year at the University of Maryland downtown in Baltimore in the evenings. While I was still a carhop, I started looking for other employment opportunities. There was an opening at the Hecht Company for a salesman in the boys' department. I applied and got that job for $45.00 a week gross ($34.00 net). The company and the people were nice, but that job was not for me.

I sold a pair of socks once in a while, but it was never busy. I was not allowed to sit down, and there was a large clock in front of me. It was extremely boring, and I got very tired of standing for eight hours, twiddling my thumbs. I was used to being active, not standing around doing nothing. The job was more stable than being a carhop; but I kept looking for another opportunity and found one at the Good Humor Ice Cream Company as a clerk/bookkeeping assistant. The salary there was $85.00 per week.

So I told my supervisor at the Hecht Co. I was leaving. She tried to talk me into staying and offered me a promotion as a window decorator, which would pay less for now, like $30.00 per week, but promotions were quite possible later. She suggested that, I, being new in this country, should not jump from job to job. *Well,* I thought, *if at anytime I can about double my pay, I should do it if all else looks good.*

I started attending the church regularly and became involved with the young people in Sunday school as well as in training union on Sunday evenings, where Linda and I would see each other, of course. There was usually a social time afterward where we would go out to either Champs, where I initially worked as a carhop, or to the Varsity, both neat local and popular eating and gathering places—especially for young people. Sometimes we'd go bowling with the whole group on Saturday nights. Linda's brother, Griff, was engaged to Marion, and they were also part of the young people's group.

We had our first date together when, one Sunday evening, I asked Linda if I could walk her home, about one mile, right after a church gathering. The only way was through a partially wooded neighborhood. I took her hand; and as we walked, we just felt a oneness that was hard to explain, except perhaps in terms of love. She still talks about my warm hand holding her cold hand. It meant so much to her, she said. She felt quite secure with me; and while holding her hand on that walk, our hearts grew closer. That event turned out to be a precursor for a marriage made in heaven—all initiated by a casual conversation with a stranger in the middle of the ocean.

When I was able to buy a car, we dated frequently. On one of our first car dates, Linda remembers that I parked the car by the Washington Monument at Mt. Vernon Place and gave her a small pair of brightly colored Dutch wooden shoes, a special time for both of us. We were getting very serious, but I was not ready for marriage—especially financially. I had a long way to go in school and a long way toward a career. So I decided it would be best for us to break up. We went to a restaurant, and I explained everything to her—that right then I could not take on the responsibility of marriage. We talked about it. She understood and perhaps expected it. But of course, it was difficult for both of us.

Well, I kept busy with school and working at the Good Humor Ice Cream Company. While Linda's grandmother was visiting one day, she heard about the breakup and noticed how sad Linda was. Her famous words of wisdom were, "If he loves you, he'll come back." She was right. Six months later, while at a restaurant with Linwood, I suddenly excused myself and called Linda. Linwood was visibly upset. Apparently he had also wanted to date Linda. Well, at that point, she had not been snatched up and we dated again.

In the summer of 1959, we decided on a November wedding at Brantly Baptist Church, even though my family could not attend. The wedding was a wonderful event. Dr. L. Tucker Gibson, the pastor, presided over the ceremony; and it was a very serious, worshipful, and most appropriate and beautiful occasion.

Linda's father, of course, gave her away. The office employees of the Good Humor Ice Cream Company attended, including the president, Mr. Stough. The law department of the Western Maryland Railway Company, where Linda worked, was well represented. Linda's

Grandmother Reese, other family members, friends, and members of Brantly and other guests were present. Immediately after the wedding, we went downstairs for the reception when we received a call from Pa and Moe in Holland. Having to answer the phone upstairs, we had to leave the reception. It was difficult for my parents, not being able to be at the wedding; but they understood that we would see them later.

Just tied the knot, 1959

After the wedding, for our honeymoon, we drove to New York City in our 1951 gray Chevrolet two-door. I had been able to buy that car for $450.00 and had paid an insurance salesman $150.00 for car insurance. We stayed at the Taft Hotel; saw a movie; saw a Broadway play, *The Flower Drum Song*; and did sightseeing. When I found out the cost to park a car at the Taft Hotel garage, I drove Linda to Long Island the next morning, parked the car on some side street, and we took the subway back to Manhattan. At the end of the honeymoon, we picked up the car again and had saved a good bit of money by not parking in the hotel garage. We had a fantastic four-day honeymoon in New York City.

After the honeymoon, we came to our newly furnished apartment in Ten Hills off Edmondson Avenue and settled in. Incidentally, when I came back to work at Good Humor, Mr. James East, my supervisor, asked me about the trip to New York. In the conversation, I mentioned that I had paid for car insurance but never obtained any paperwork or certificate. Well, he called the state insurance commissioner, and the next day, the insurance salesman came to where I worked with $150.00 in cash. He told me that he was sorry, but he was unable to get the car insurance for me. Then he just walked off.

Mr. East knew what had happened, that insurance salesman had tried to take advantage of a new immigrant. He was going to pocket the money for himself. So we had gone to New York without any car insurance. It was a good thing we didn't have an accident.

Linda and I had great goals, and we worked hard. On the street near our apartment, we would often pass each other, as Linda would be coming home from work while I would just be leaving for night school. Linda was very supportive of me and my efforts to become a success in the United States.

Because my parents in Holland were unable to attend our wedding, Linda insisted that we try to bring them over for a visit the following summer. So we saved up to pay for school, and we saved up to pay for my parents' visit as well. And visit they did. They stayed with us in our apartment the next summer. It was great to be able to pick them up in New York from the ship, the *Maasdam*, and bring them to Baltimore. They not only met Linda for the first time but her parents and family too. It was just terrific. We were in a relatively roomy second-floor apartment on North Chapel Gate Lane, and my parents could comfortably stay with us.

A few weeks into my parents' visit, we suddenly received notice that we had to move. The landlady had other plans for our place. Pa and Moe became rather upset and almost frightened. They thought that it would be extremely difficult for us to find another place to rent. In Holland, which is very densely populated, the housing situation is still quite difficult. One has to apply to rent an apartment, has to place one's name on a waiting list, and then has to wait sometimes as long as two years.

I tried to assure Pa and Moe that this was not such a problem here. We went to a new apartment development, Wakefield at Tucker Lane, and found out that a good number of apartments were available. I said to Pa and Moe, "How many apartments would you like to rent here today?" They were just amazed. No waiting list? No rental housing shortages? They could hardly believe it. They enjoyed their visit, and we hated to see them leave.

After my first two years of studies, I had enough semester credits to be a sophomore. I left Good Humor Ice Cream and started selling cookware door to door for Wear-Ever Aluminum so that during the day I could attend the University of Maryland at College Park full time. I took care of my cookware selling responsibilities in the evenings and on weekends as time allowed. Selling was a good experience for me because I learned how to deal with the public. This was important because I would eventually need to deal with dental patients.

In the meantime, Linda continued working as a secretary at the Western Maryland Railway Company. By putting our incomes together, we managed. During marriage counseling, Dr. Gibson gave us some good advice. He said that after marriage, it's no longer "my" money and "your" money, but "our" money. I have never forgotten that; and it has worked out well for Linda and me. (As it was stated during our wedding, "The two shall become one.")

It was at College Park that I had some real hurdles to overcome. The first courses I took in inorganic chemistry and physics were very difficult. To look at two glasses of water and call one basic and the other acidic made no sense to me. They looked the same. By the time I found out the difference, the courses were over, and I had flunked.

I went back to Dr. Vandenbosche and shared my troubles with him. I was pretty disappointed, to say the least, if not downright depressed. During the course of college and, later, dental school, such setbacks occurred at least three times. And when I thought it was over, that I was just not meant to be a dentist and I'd better abandon such plans, I'd walk into Dr. Vandenbosche's office. It was the craziest thing. I'd share my troubles with him; he'd listen intently; and each time, after about fifteen or twenty minutes, I'd walk out of his office and be totally turned around. Confident and with my chest out, I felt as if I could conquer the world and everything would be okay. I still do not know what he said. He never gave me anything except hope, self-confidence, and the psychological strength to go on and try harder. It worked every time. It was just incredible. Apparently, Dr. Vandenbosche was very knowledgeable about people. He was the perfect man to be dean of admissions.

Sadly, a year after I graduated from dental school, he passed away. His son, Raoul, knew of my admiration for his father; and he asked me if I would be one of the pallbearers at his funeral. It was an honor; but at that point in my life, it was the most difficult thing I had ever done. It was as if I had lost my own father. That entire day, I fought back tears, mostly unsuccessfully.

U.S. CITIZEN!

As soon as I could, after five years as a legal alien, I applied for citizenship; and on June 12, 1964, I became a naturalized citizen of the United States of America. What a great moment that was for me! It was a real-dream-come-true. At that time, I also officially changed my name from Jan van den Berge to John Vandenberge, Americanized.

In Holland, my name was listed alphabetically in the phone book under *B* (Berge). When my parents arrived in New York City, we had a hard time finding their luggage on the pier. It was placed with the *V's* (Vandenberge) instead of with the *B's*. So I thought that changing my name would be more practical.

While in dental school, I was honored to be the vice president of the freshman class after Wayne Lopez, a classmate who had become my friend, had introduced me as a candidate for election. I also was vice president of the sophomore class and became president of the junior class. I was really honored to be the president of the student senate during my senior year. Only in the United States!

As president of the student senate, I was responsible for making announcements to the dental school classes. On one such occasion, I announced that there would be a lecture on general anesthesia and intravenous sedation in dentistry at the Alcazar Hotel in downtown Baltimore one evening. All students of the junior and senior classes were invited. It was free of charge. Dr. Leonard Monheim from Pittsburgh, a nationally renowned dental hospital anesthesiologist, and Dr. Sylvan M. Shane from Baltimore, also a dentist and hospital anesthesiologist, were the speakers.

When the evening came, although there were other community dentists in attendance, I was the only student from the dental school who attended. It was a most interesting lecture. Afterward, I contacted Dr. Shane, and he invited me to come and see him work at his office on Mountain Road in Pasadena, Maryland. I became quite interested in this field because I knew there were a lot of people who were afraid to go to the dentist—more so than today.

Eventually, I applied for a year of hospital dental anesthesiology residency training at the University of Pittsburgh with Dr. Leonard Monheim and Dr. Peter Safar, also a very well-known medical anesthesiologist, and I was accepted. So after graduation I took Linda and our two sons, John and Reese, with me to live in an apartment in Pittsburgh, Pennsylvania, during my year of hospital anesthesia residency training.

I was very encouraged by Dr. Sylvan Shane, whom I admire as a professional and a friend. He is retired now. He had great skills and was very knowledgeable as an anesthesiologist. He was able to put very frightened patients to sleep safely and effectively. It was a wonderful year of learning. I put patients to sleep at the Veterans Hospital, the Children's Hospital, and the Presbyterian University Hospital in Pittsburgh. I gained experience putting little children to sleep as well as adults and geriatric patients. Some of the older patients were ninety-five years old and older, including some Spanish-American War Veterans who were very good, very tough patients.

In 1967 I graduated from the Baltimore College of Dental Surgery. I was very happy that my parents could attend my graduation from dental school. Pa had been disappointed that I did not get more education in Holland. I was fortunate enough to be able to become a dentist, even if it was, perhaps, the hard and long way. It was neat that my parents also got to see the commencement speaker, Mr. Hubert H. Humphrey, the vice president of the United States at the time. I completed the anesthesia training in Pittsburgh in May 1968 and began a dental practice in Arbutus near Baltimore in the fall of 1968.

Dental School Graduation (with Pa and Moe, 1967)

CHAPTER 11

CHURCH, POLITICS, HEALTH, FAMILY, AND MIRACLES

My church attendance history has become richer with time. Serving in church reminds me of Pa telling me that he was an usher doing the collection many years ago. He had to maneuver a long pole with a bag at the end, and this was positioned in front of each parishioner for them to place their offering into the bag. As he held the bag in front of his brother Jacob, sitting in the pew, Jacob held on to the tassel at the bottom of the bag, looking straight ahead with a very serious expression on his face, so Pa could not pull the pole and bag back until Jacob let go. Pa pulled, and finally Jacob let go.

Then there was a time when one of our sons had a dollar to put into the offering plate at church. He had the dollar bill in his pocket all morning, and it had gotten pretty wrinkled and crumpled up. So when the usher, Mr. Garland Rosson, the banker, was ready to receive our son's dollar, our son was embarrassed to put it in the offering plate all wrinkled, so he tried to flatten it out as best he could while Mr. Rosson was waiting in the aisle. Finally, Mr. Rosson gently leaned over to him and said, "Do you want me to get you a steam iron?"

Later we joined Trinity Assembly of God Church in Lutherville, near Baltimore, where we stayed for a few years. We did not get involved as volunteers there. One incident stands out in my memory, though. One Sunday evening we went to Trinity to attend a music worship service. There was no sermon, no message, but just worshipful music led by Rev. Tom McDonald. Linda and I did not expect anything special. We just went to worship God.

When I walked in, I was limping slightly because my one knee had been hurting quite badly and I was scheduled to see the orthopedic surgeon the next day, Monday, to see what could be done about it. During the service, I did not notice anything unusual. However, as we walked out after the service had ended, I said to Linda, "Guess what. My knee is not hurting!" I could hardly believe it.

Outside, in the parking lot, I jogged a little, jumped up and down a little, and nothing hurt. My knee has not hurt like that again, and I did not need to go to the surgeon the next day. What a sensation to realize that God, who looks after an awful lot of people, would touch my knee and heal it, even when I was not expecting it. There was just no other explanation.

PREVENTIVE HEALTH

In March of 1996, I received a phone call from a friend who told me there was a very interesting lecture on health and nutrition taking place in a church in Silver Spring, Maryland. He knew of my interest in preventive medicine and health in general. I thought that would be just another boring lecture on diets and did not want to go. But then I realized I should attend anyway. One never knows what one can learn.

The speaker was Dr. George Malkmus from Tennessee who had colon cancer some twenty-two years ago. His mother had died of colon cancer two years earlier. She was a registered nurse, did everything the doctors told her to do, received chemotherapy, radiation, and surgery, but died a horrible death two years before Dr. Malkmus, himself, was diagnosed with a baseball-sized malignant tumor on his transverse colon. Dr. Malkmus, a very busy Baptist minister with successful church and radio programs in New York State, went to God and asked what was going on. After all, he was working for God and now faced the prospect of dying as his mother did.

He knew that he did not want to take the chemotherapy treatments because he believed that those treatments actually had killed his mother. He did a lot of research and finally found an evangelist from Texas, Lester Roloff, who told George to take a year and eat nothing but vegetables and drink their juices as well as fruits and fruit juices. George did just that; and after one year, the tumor was totally gone and other symptoms disappeared as well. That was quite a convincing story as he explained his diet recommendations and rationale. I came away from that meeting with a real determination to follow his advice. I changed my diet the next morning.

Linda said, "You are ruining my life! A total diet change and no more coffee?" (She is a great cook and really enjoys cooking.) I have been on that regimen since March of 1996 and have not had one headache since. I used to get about three bad headaches a month—some were so bad that I had to go to bed and stay home from work. I also have had no colds, except once when we were on vacation and I went off the diet, figuring one week wouldn't make much difference. Well, it did. I got a terrible cold. I have not had any other colds or flus, even though people around me have. (One recent exception: I had a strange, low-grade bronchitis, but no cold as such.) This has been just amazing and wonderful. So I have become basically a vegetarian, although I do eat some salmon and sardines occasionally and take some supplemental vitamins and B-12 shots. In addition, I exercise regularly to stay healthy. Linda and I are basically on that same diet, although she doesn't mind "jumping ship" once in a while. This diet, called the Hallelujah Diet, is now being used worldwide by well over one million people with many incredible testimonies.[2] It may not be for everybody, but it surely works for me.

In 1996, I started the Natural Health Forum because of my interest in preventive health. With the full cooperation of Rev. Ben Boggess at the local Seventh Day Adventist Church in Ellicott City, we held monthly meetings at his church auditorium. We attracted people from the community who expressed an interest in improving their personal health. We invited experts in different health specialties as guest speakers. We produced a monthly newsletter and had a lot of fun doing it as we all learned. The program is on hold for now. In 1997, Linda and I attended the Hallelujah Acres three-day seminar with Dr. George Malkmus, which qualified us as health ministers with them.

CHURCH EXPERIENCES

A very interesting thing happened after we left Chapelgate Presbyterian Church, where we had been for about two years. Linda and I just did not know which church to join next. We prayed, but we did not receive an answer or direction from the Lord.

So one cold, wintry Sunday morning, somewhat frustrated, we prayed again, praising God and thanking him and asking for his plan for us. We stood in the living room of our apartment, my arm around Linda's shoulders, in front of the balcony glass door. We had closed our eyes and were waiting on the Lord.

We know from past experience that sometimes God speaks to us in a small, soft voice, which is like hearing a thought. This is how Opa van den Berge and others in the family had heard from God at times. In a way, it is mysterious; but on the other hand, it is very real. God speaks in various ways to people; some hear thoughts or his voice; and others hear from him through circumstances, dreams or visions, or words from the Scriptures; and, of course, all must conform to the written Word of the Bible. God is very creative, not limited to any one way of doing things.

So what happened this time? Suddenly we heard some tapping sounds on the sliding glass balcony door window. We opened our eyes, and to our great surprise (we could hardly believe what we saw), sitting all across the top of the metal balcony railing, there were cute, dark brown, puffy, medium-sized birds, exactly equidistant from one another, about one inch or less apart. They were facing us, just staring at us. Then we saw some other birds, just like these, fly toward the balcony window, some tapping on the window as if to say, "Won't you let us come in?"

We had never seen more than one or two birds at a time on the balcony before this time or since. These birds were not sparrows. They were bigger and certainly a lot smaller than crows. We have never seen them, before or after. After a short time, as if by a signal from somewhere, they all flew off at once. Linda and I just stood there, amazed. We knew that this was something different and special. It seemed that the Lord said through that experience, "If He cares for and guides those birds, He will surely care for and guide us".

This reminded us that the Bible says that "not one sparrow falls to the ground without God noticing it" (Matthew 10:29) and that we are of "more value than many sparrows" (Matthew 10:31). "Don't you think I can take care of you and guide you as well?" (Psalm 48:14), for this God, our God forever and ever; he will be our guide, even to death.

On the next Sunday, we knew somehow that we were supposed to visit Bishop Cummins Memorial Church in Catonsville. We enjoyed being at that church, especially after we met the Rector, Rev. Dr. Paul Chaim Schenck, a Jewish-Christian believer who received us warmly. We knew this was God's answer.

We stayed there from 1997 to 2004, and I became very much involved, serving as usher, vestryman, executive committee member, licensed layreader, teacher, Sunday school superintendent, and as a prayer counselor. The pastor, or rector as he is called in the Reformed Episcopal Church, and I became good friends. He is a remarkable man, even-tempered, very wise, mature, and learned.

On recommendation and at the insistence of some friendly pastors, I applied for ordination to be a minister with the Independent Assemblies of God, International, in California. I received the ordination in 1995. Then, in 2004, I also received the ordination as a Presbyter with the Methodist Episcopal Church USA. The ceremony was held at Bishop Cummins Memorial Church, Rev. Rob Schenck presiding. What a wonderful job he did!

Afterward, we discovered a problem. The bishop of the Reformed Episcopal Church sent an e-mail to Bishop Cummins Memorial Church saying that since I was now ordained in another denomination, I had forfeited my membership in the Reformed Episcopal Church and could no longer function in any official capacity. What a shock that was!

I forgave the bishop, resigned, and then was invited to become a chaplain with Rev. Rob Schenck's ministry in Washington, DC, under the banner of the Methodist Episcopal Church USA (MECUSA) Church, Faith and Action Ministry and The National Clergy Council. This ministry witnesses and ministers to those who determine public policy and provides spiritual help in the form of church services, Bible studies, and prayer services. As of this writing, I am in the early stage of this ministry and am eagerly looking forward to what the Lord has in store for us there.

Very recently, I was quite honored to receive the Honorary Doctor of Divinity Degree by the Methodist Episcopal Church USA at Georgetown University in Washington, DC, on recommendation of the Mid-Atlantic Conference Joint Academic Commission and the National Clergy Council Board of Scholars.

The Rev. David Moshier, Conferral, at right and the Honorable Judge Randy Rogers, assisting, at left.

Receiving an Honorary Doctorate of Divinity, MECUSA

A UNIQUE GRANDFATHER

Many unusual things happened with Opa van den Berge, my father's father. For example, in Rotterdam, there was a man who apparently had unusual powers of discernment. He would come on stage at a local theater and would ask for someone to come forward to ask about a lost relative or something like that. He would ask for a personal item, like keys. He would start meditating while feeling the keys and then tell the person where their distant relative was and what he or she was doing and whether he or she was alive or not. The younger generation was quite excited about this, including Opa's sons. He was performing every night for a week. After Monday's performance, the sons asked Opa to come and see. He would not go. They asked him every night trying to convince him to join them. He would not go, but finally, on Friday night, the last night, he agreed and did go. He sat in the middle of the audience with his sons and watched. The man came on stage, introduced himself, said what he was going to do; but then he got quiet, started perspiring, and could not perform. He paced up and down the stage, kept perspiring, seemed confused, and remained quiet until he stopped, looked at the audience intently and said, "There is someone here who is against me!" Opa stood up and said, "I'll go," and left. After Opa left, the performance went on just fine. The point, of course, is that the man did not have a godly gift; it was demonic. The Spirit of God in Opa was too strong for the spirit in that man. Opa knew exactly what was going on and explained it later to his children, I'm sure.

Great miracles seemed to flow through Opa. Pa, on the other hand, had other gifts. He was a wonderfully compassionate, gentle man who had no enemies. As a matter of fact, his enemies became friends, as was pointed out earlier with the two Nazi physicians who came to visit for tea and brought my mother flowers. The Bible says, "When a man's ways please the Lord, he makes even his enemies at peace with him," (Proverbs 16:7). That was my father! He loved the compassionate part of his work where he would find suitable employment for handicapped people. He was very successful at that.

John Griffith, our eldest son is probably the most outgoing of our sons, though a quiet, determined person with a charming, disarming personality. He loves children and was very good at teaching sports to his brothers. He graduated from the University of Maryland and from Ohio Northern Law School, worked for an insurance company but then decided to start his own business. He purchased a couple of vending machines and serviced them at night and on weekends. He worked hard at becoming his own boss and succeeded, having his own full-time vending machine business now called Maryland Vending.

Rebecca, his lovely wife, a registered nurse, switched careers, working now with Party-Lite, and she is doing very well. She helps with the vending business also. At the time of this writing, they have two sons, John Marco and Simon William, more gifts from God.

Our second-born son, Reese, a graduate of the University of Baltimore, working at UPS is very talented and creative with gardening and woodwork skills. He enjoys playing soccer, is a real people person, has many friends and is fun to be around . He was a lot of help during the campaigns and has always been very supportive of what I have been doing. He is a very loyal, Christian man. We are very proud of him as we are of all our sons.

Martin is a graduate of Towson State University. He became an excellent teacher in the Baltimore County School System and is now the assistant principal at Hammond High School in Howard County. He and his lovely wife, Becky, have two children, Tyler (Alan) and Tori (Victoria Ann). Martin, a quiet, pensive person, is a solid Christian family man who is loyal to God and country. He is very observant. He is now a great coach at home and a very fine husband and father. He and I enjoy playing tennis whenever we can, which is not so often anymore because family obligations come first. Years ago, I could beat him regularly; but one year in April, he told me that he was not going to shave until he beat me. It was not until August in Ocean City, when he got his father on a court on a very, very hot and humid day that he finally won a tennis match. I have so much fun competing in friendly games with all of our sons, especially when we all play soccer or tennis.The exercise, the fellowship, and the bonding are the important things.

Alan, the youngest, is another wonderful son and is goodhearted with an engaging personality. He is quite athletic – played baseball in high school as a very fine pitcher and he plays soccer very well. Alan, a very talented landscaper by trade, has now joined in partnership with John with Maryland Vending. His lovely wife, Jennifer, is a professional speech therapist at a large nursing home facility in the Baltimore area. She and Alan have a daughter, Alyssa Faith, and a son, Blake Michael.

CHAPTER 12
FORTY YEARS OF DENTISTRY AND FAMILY LIFE

I will always appreciate the opportunity I had to become a dentist in the United States. During the first twelve years or so, I did a good deal of sedation dentistry, which involves putting patients to sleep who are fearful about having their teeth filled or extracted. At three hospitals in Pittsburgh, I learned to administer anesthesia safely; and then later—once I came back to Baltimore to start a general dentistry practice in Arbutus—I worked part-time with Dr. Sylvan Shane in Pasadena. I learned a lot from him. He was my mentor and friend. The patient's safety was always his highest priority. Together, we had a tremendous safety record—not one fatality that I know of.

Each of us had at least one patient we had to send to the hospital. Dr. Shane had a patient who had a badly abscessed tooth that needed to be extracted. She was quite apprehensive and gave a very short, negative medical history. Dr. Shane extracted the tooth under sedation anesthesia. Everything went fine except that when she woke up and he sat her up, she lost consciousness. When he leaned the chair back down, she woke up. He put her back up, she passed out.

He noticed that he could bring her in and out of consciousness by lifting her up and putting her back in the lying-down position. This meant that she could not go home in an unconscious state. Dr. Shane called in the son of the patient, a man of about forty-five to fifty years of age. Dr. Shane said to him, "Tell me about your mother. Has she been sick lately or anything like that?" The son said that she had just been released from a hospital "less than two weeks ago."

She did not want to tell Dr. Shane about it, thinking he might not extract the tooth. So Dr. Shane called the ambulance and spoke with the cardiologist at the hospital, who did blood tests on her, etc. He found out that her potassium level was so low that her heart was seriously deficient. She was treated successfully and soon went home. Dr. Shane and I were occasionally on the phone with each other on such cases. He was like a medical detective who had a way of figuring out complicated situations.

John the dentist

One of the most interesting cases I had was a thirty-seven-year-old lady who needed a filling in an upper bicuspid tooth (without intravenous sedation) and she received local anesthesia—a routine case, I thought. But that wasn't so. Upon injecting the first drops of xylocaine with epinephrine, a standard anesthetic, I noticed that her gum in the injected area became very white, unusually so. I withdrew the syringe, immediately after which she said she was not feeling well.

She started breathing heavily and said she sensed everything leaving her extremities and centering in her heart area. Then I noticed that her arms became pale as well as her face and legs. This is called central pooling, where the blood gets concentrated around vital organs, such as the heart. She started complaining that she could not breathe even though she was exchanging air pretty well.

I reclined her completely to lessen any stress on her heart and started giving her oxygen. I prepared an intravenous line in her arm and gave her Solu-Cortef, a cortisone-type drug, because I realized she had gone or was going into anaphylactic shock. I had seen it in the hospital. I also gave her Benadryl as an anti-allergy medication, as well as intravenous fluids. I continued to talk with her, encourage her, and reassure her that she was okay and would be okay.

After about half an hour, I slowly sat her up because her breathing had become regular. As soon as I did, her labored breathing and the strange feeling in her chest started again, so I leaned the dental chair back down immediately. This went on for another forty-five minutes before I could finally sit her up. She felt very weak.

I figured she was either allergic or very sensitive to the xylocaine or the synthetic Epinephrine. Later, I called the obstetrician who had recently delivered her fourth child, and he said he had used xylocaine without Epinephrine. So there was my answer: she was very sensitive to synthetic Epinephrine. This was a rare and life-threatening situation. My anesthesia training came in handy for any patient, of course, but especially for this patient because she was my wife, Linda.

I have yet to hear or read of another dentist who has had a similar experience. It turns out that to this day, Linda is very sensitive to any drug. She usually needs half or less of any normal dose.

I distinctly remember a situation some thirty-five years ago when a little girl, about age five, was brought in by her parents, kicking and screaming. When the dental assistant came to my office to tell me that the next patient was there, I told her "I know. I can hear her." Her parents could not control her except to bring her into the waiting room. They asked me to take care of her, no matter what it took. It was, "Whatever you can do. Go ahead, Doc!" Well, I picked her up, gently, by her arms and put her in the dental chair. She could not stop screaming. What to do?

I had read about the "blue baby" technique in a textbook and thought it was the right situation to try it. I placed my hand over her mouth to stop her from screaming so that I could communicate with her. With this technique, the child does not actually turn blue because she can breathe through her nose. I told her that she was a good girl but perhaps not behaving correctly. When I moved my hand off of her mouth, she screamed, "No! I am a bad girl!"

Anyway, we rescheduled after I assessed what needed to be done. At a subsequent appointment, she was brought in, and we put her to sleep to repair all her little black stubs that were once nice-looking white teeth. Her mother had been putting sugar in her bottle at night so she would sleep better.

Three months later, the family came back so I could check and see how the little girl was doing. I wondered how she would react since I had covered her mouth. She had gone through a difficult patient management episode. To my surprise, as soon as she saw me, she ran to me, jumped in my arms, and hugged me. She was so happy to see me, apparently. Once seated, I asked her how she was doing. I asked her what she remembered about the last appointments. She did not remember anything negative. I guess this form of tough love worked.

This was the only time that I have used that "blue baby" technique. One cannot use this today, of course, because one would quickly be accused of child abuse. Well, I know the child was not abused at all; and I think I did her and her parents a big service. I reminded the child at the last appointment that she was a good girl. She agreed. We always got along really well.

I have had the privilege of meeting many wonderful patients and some I still see today. Dentistry does not appeal, as a career, to many people; but the most gratifying part is when a patient is in severe pain and I can help them find relief from pain and/or infections.

For me, there is also a spiritual side to dentistry. In one of our offices in Catonsville, we occupied two floors and had a staff of six, including another dentist. Downstairs, we had a conference room where we met as a staff each morning some fifteen minutes before we saw the first patient. We reviewed the schedule for the day, made some observations, and then we had a short prayer. I usually prayed for wisdom for all of us; protection for the patients and ourselves; and, in general, asked the Lord's blessings on the day.

One day, I thought, driving to the office, *I wonder what the staff really thinks of my saying a prayer each morning.* I did not want it to be a requirement, like, "The boss says we are praying, so everyone has to because the boss says so." So we discussed the prayer we say each morning, the meaning of it, and the possible benefits of it, but we did not actually pray.

Once, some forty years ago, someone broke into my office in Arbutus during the night and tried to steal drugs or syringes with needles. Not much was stolen; and we did not pray as a staff in the morning. Otherwise, since we prayed each morning, no mishaps ever occurred again in forty years; except this one morning we did not actually pray. During the staff meeting at lunchtime downstairs, some man came in the office upstairs, distracted the front desk person, and stole the girls' pocketbooks. What a shock!

The next morning, we got together and I asked the staff, "Shall we pray or just discuss prayer?" There was a very firm, unanimous response: "Pray!" No more break-ins have occurred after that. We thank God for the protection. I am sure other dentists and physicians pray as well, but it is not discussed very often.

CHRISTIAN AND PROFESSIONAL POLITICS

For some reason, I have always been attracted to politics, which is grounded in my love for this country and what it stands for. I had to go to the "land of the free and the home of the brave." It automatically carried me into the rest of my life. I was in dental politics in school and ran for public political office twice; but in between, I was involved in Christian politics.

In 1980, I was privileged to be the co-state coordinator for "Washington for Jesus" and from 1982–1984, I was the Maryland State coordinator for "The Freedom Council," which was the forerunner of "The Christian Coalition." Both organizations were founded by Dr. Pat Robertson. I have always believed that it is very important for Christians to be involved in politics. Their voices need to be heard up to the highest levels in government, because they can represent God's wisdom and direction for people in any elected or appointed office. The kings living in the times of the Old Testament usually leaned on and acted wisely on the advice of the prophets.

In dental politics, I was privileged to serve on a number of committees and organizations. I pleasantly recall being the president of the Maryland Dental Society of Anesthesiology, Inc. from 1972–1979; and from 1976–1981, I was a member of the fellowship committee of the American Dental Society of Anesthesiology, Inc. This committee met during the winter dental meetings in Chicago. Our assignment there each year was to examine general dentists and oral surgeons who were candidates for the anesthesiology fellowship. We needed to make sure they were well qualified to be putting dental patients to sleep safely in their dental offices.

This was an assignment we took very seriously; and not every candidate passed the exam, which was mostly an oral interview. We placed them in some hypothetical, clinical, and emergency situations to see what they would do to prevent accidents and catastrophes. I might add that the safety record of dentists putting patients to sleep for dental procedures is excellent and has been for many years.

In 1979 Governor Hughes of Maryland signed a bill into law for general anesthesia permits for dentists in Maryland, which our ad-hoc committee on state anesthesia laws had submitted. This bill certainly helped to maintain the high safety record of Maryland dentists relative to general anesthesia and intravenous sedation. Dentists in Maryland regularly take continuing education courses to maintain their state-issued dental licenses, as I do as well.

HOLLAND VISIT

One thing I was able to do was visit Holland as a dentist in 1985 with Linda and our four sons. It was a very memorable trip. I had not been there since 1958 and felt a little strange the first day, even in Rotterdam, my hometown.

Some things seemed the same, but a lot had changed. In the middle of the second day, all of a sudden, a lot of things just clicked. I knew my way around again. It all came back. I had rented a VW bus in Rotterdam; and we went to a good number of historic places, such as Delft, where I used to live; and the Hague, Zierikzee, the polders with windmills, and Volendam.

My cousin, Willie van den Berge, had arranged a very nice travel plan for us, including old hotels to stay in so we could taste the real Dutch atmosphere. For example, in Zierikzee we stayed in a quaint hotel, Mondragon. Zierikzee has a drawbridge, a castle, an old marketplace in front of the big church. It is very picturesque and historic.

Windmills never change

John Vandenberge and his family, 1985, in Holland

Linda especially loved it. Zierikzee has a history closer to home than we then knew. The museum in Zierikzee has a plaque that caught Linda's eye. It commemorates the early Dutch settlement in Lewes, Delaware (Swanendael). It says:

One in Christ
to the Glory Of God and in Memory of
Pieter Cornelius Plockroy Zierikzee
67.
A Pioneer of Christian Civilization
in America
Founder of the Dutch Colony
Swaanendael, Delaware, USA
The Netherlands Society of Philadelphia
Rears this Memorial
September, 1913

Zwaanendaal House, a museum in Lewes, Delaware, is a smaller scale adaptation of the town hall at Hoorn, Netherlands (Holland), ancestral home of the original Dutch settlers of Lewes.[3]

Hoorn is a seaport in North Holland, on a bay of the IJsselmeer (also called Zuiderzee) called Hoornerhop, twenty-three miles northeast of Amsterdam. In 1356, it received municipal privileges, and it was surrounded by walls. In 1416, the first great net was made for fishery.

Zierikzee was so picturesque with the castle at the entrance to the town and a moat around it. There was a little wooden drawbridge we crossed to get into town; and then we saw a very large, beautifully landscaped center plaza strip. There were shops on both sides of the strip and rows of homes with Hotel Mondragon in between. At the end of the plaza across the street was an outdoor restaurant where we had coffee and delicious Dutch pastries, which I remembered fondly from years ago when I lived in Holland. It was like stepping into the eighteenth century.

Zierikzee, bridge over the canal

The town continued on both sides of the street, which were filled with tourists, shoppers, and an old-fashioned street organ that was making lovely music. When I was a boy, the street organ was pulled by a horse; but this one was pulled by a Mercedes. The attendees moved the organ from street to street, soliciting donations with a tin cup that they shook in rhythm with the music while the Dutch dolls danced to the music—quite a nice attraction.

On a one-way street, we found a Christian bookstore on the second floor, where we attended a worship service, in Dutch, on Sunday morning. We found that one Christian word seems to be the same in all languages—*hallelujah*—which literally means "Praise ye the Lord!"

We visited a lot of stores in the Lijnbaan in Rotterdam, and we went to city hall. I showed the family where Churchill and Queen Wilhelmina stood on the city hall balcony after the war. We also visited Amsterdam, where we went to the Rijksmuseum to see famous paintings, The Night Watch by Rembrandt being one of them. We learned that this very famous painting, which is quite large, was hidden during the war and moved three times. The Nazis never found it, even though they were looking for it. We also toured the canals in Amsterdam.

I have a very warm spot in my heart for Holland. It will always be my "home country" in the sense that I was raised there; went through the war; and regained freedom because some wonderful people, Americans and Canadians, brought it to us. My ancestors are buried there, and some relatives still live there. I regret to see some negative aspects of current life in Holland, but hopefully that will change for the better.

I did return to Rotterdam with Linda in January of 2009, as I was asked to perform the funeral service for my brother, Martin. It was a very sad and difficult experience because Martin and I were so close and had gone through the war together.

Gayle, Martin's wife, as an American, adjusted well to Holland and was a great support for Martin. Unfortunately, Gayle had a stroke as did Martin later and they moved to Akropolis, a wonderful assisted living-type place where Gayle lives now in Rotterdam.

GOVERNMENTAL POLITICS

In 1980, I became a booster for the United States and became motivated to help because some things had not been going right for us as a country. I was excited about Mr. Ronald Reagan's campaign for the presidency. I had become a republican and wanted to help my country. So I went to Annapolis and signed up to be a candidate for the state legislature.

After I talked with some friends and received some encouragement, we prayed about it and felt it was the right thing for me to do. We printed a sheet of paper that spelled out the things that I was in favor of and the things I was against. As much as we could, we distributed that piece of paper door to door and through the mail. I won the primary, to the surprise of many people, especially local Republicans and the media, who did not know who I was.

Ready for a parade

I had not participated in the local Republican Party before, and I should have, but then I did join and became involved in the party's activities. And I enjoyed it very much because it was for a great cause. I did not win the general election, but it was a lot of fun, very educational, and I felt I had done the right thing. Many wonderful people, especially my family, were very supportive, and I am very grateful for that.

Later, in 1986, I ran again, this time for the US Congress, Sixth District in Maryland. Again, winning the primary, I expected to win the general election, but it did not happen. That race cost us quite a bit of money and was financially painful for us. We almost went bankrupt. Though difficult, these campaigns were interesting experiences to go through.

I met President Ronald Reagan and had a very nice, short conversation with him. During the campaign, there was a meeting at Festival Hall in Baltimore (where the convention center is now) where President Reagan spoke. Afterward, there was a restricted area where some people got to meet the president. I was not on the list, even though I was a congressional candidate. However, a wonderful lady, Mrs. Marjorie Holt, the Congresswoman from Maryland's Eastern Shore First District, spotted me and thought I should be meeting the president, and she got me in for the short meeting and photo. Mr. Reagan asked what I was doing, and he was so encouraging and positive after I told him my plans. What a fine gentleman he was, and what a superb visionary optimist he was. He was quite a role model.

President Reagan and John, 1986

THANK YOU, AMERICA

I must note that this country helped get rid of Hitler and helped Holland get back on her feet with the Marshall Plan. But I also understand that Holland was one of the first countries to pay back all her debts to the United States, which I think is great. Some Dutch people appreciate America. One such person is André Rieu.

Linda and I attended his concert on May 14, 2005, in Baltimore at the First Mariner Arena. We were not sure what to expect but were very pleasantly surprised. André is from the Dutch province of Limburg in South Holland. He has a great Dutch sense of humor and uses it well. His group of outstanding musicians and vocalists gave a superb concert. Toward the end, he expressed his gratitude for the United States. He noted that sixty years earlier, Americans liberated Holland from the Nazis. He said, "We will never forget it." This was the first time that I heard a Dutch representative on any official public level say that he was grateful to the Americans. I really appreciated that heartfelt, positive gesture.

Then the orchestra did a most beautiful rendition of "America the Beautiful." It really touched my heart. Sadly, many West Europeans have been rather critical of the United States and, apparently, have forgotten how many of our soldiers died for their freedom as well.

LINDA

My wife has been my mainstay for fifty wonderful years. She is my partner; lover; the mother of our four great sons; and my corrector, editor, and stabilizer.

Linda and I love each other for life. If we have had any disagreements, they were few and far between and not memorable. We love each other too much to be "on the outs" but settle things as they occur. We've never discussed divorce. It's just not an option. She's been able to put up with me for about fifty years now, in spite of some difficult times, such as losing two political campaigns and almost going bankrupt. She is very honest and quite genuine. There's no pretense in her. There is also no mean bone in her body. She has a very discerning spirit, more than I have.

Linda is, above all, a Christian lady. Her primary goal in life, as a teenager, was to become a Christian homemaker, have a family, and be a good mother to her children. She did just that and did a great job! The boys may not always have appreciated it when they were young, but they respected her.

When we lived in Ellicott City in the house on St. John's Lane, we noticed that sometimes this duck flew into the bushes in front of the house. Soon, one of our sons hollered, "Mom, look!" There was the mother duck coming out of the bushes with twelve little ducklings in line after her. They went around the house, over the driveway, down on the grass, and into the backyard to the pond, which was down the hill at the end of our property. They just knew what to do in that pond. They were happy, obviously.

Father duck also appeared, and the parents were officially named Xerxes and Matilda. It was quite an attraction for the whole neighborhood. Dr. Castellano, Linda's obstetrician who lived a block or so away, came over to look at the ducks, and I questioned him as to why he and his profession made such a big deal about delivering babies, whereas this mother delivered twelve without any medical or veterinary help whatsoever. Watching those ducks was a daily attraction and a great experience for the boys and us.

Leaving St. Johns Lane wasn't without its surprises. Cleaning everything from top to bottom, such as people do when they leave one place to move to another, we found a bunch of wooden spoons behind a bookcase. Those were the discipline instruments we used—sparingly, I might add. Raising four boys was no picnic, of course. Linda certainly took the brunt of all the daily activities.

When I say that she's a lady, I really mean it. I love it that she is very feminine. She much prefers to wear dresses than slacks; and the more feminine a dress or blouse is, the better she likes it, and I do too. She enjoys being a girl, as the song goes from *The Flower Drum Song*, the play we saw on our honeymoon in New York City. She tries to be proper at all times and knows ethics and manners quite well. When the stresses of life come on us, however, we can do some undesirable things. I remember once when something had happened to make Linda quite upset, she really lost her cool and her control of being a lady and suddenly blurted out, "Pickles!"

Seriously, she is also a real servant. She loves to help people and is quite an excellent counselor when someone wants her advice. She is well grounded in the Scriptures and has a great deal of wisdom in discerning between good and evil, right and wrong. Anyone who is willing to take the time to get to know her will find out what a marvelous lover of people she is.

She was so much help to me. I was able to use her considerable secretarial skills. She left the Western Maryland Railway Company as a legal secretary when we were expecting our first son, and she was able to stay home with the children. She did much typing and correcting of my term papers at the university and the dental school and other business correspondence related to the dental practice later. She worked in the office for a while, doing bookkeeping, payroll, paying bills, typing letters, etc.

Linda is also an incurable romantic. She wants to travel and see America and Israel. We enjoy ballroom dancing on occasion; and she loves romantic music, such as Glenn Miller, Perry Como, Bing Crosby, etc. Her favorite is Christian music that brings us closer to God in times of worship. She is a gem, and I am very grateful to God for leading me to her. The Bible says, "But a prudent wife is from the Lord" (Proverbs 19:14b); and "He who finds a wife finds a good thing…" (Proverbs 18:22a); and, as if a bonus, "And obtains favor from the Lord" (Proverbs 18:22b).

CHAPTER 13
FEATURES OF MY TWO FAMILIES

Having come from Holland to America, I had basically started a new life with great uncertainties. One goes through questions such as, Where did I come from and where am I going? Did I do the right thing going to America? How will I fit in, and where do I go and what do I do? So what kind of a Dutch family did I come from, and which kind of an American family did I eventually marry into?

From the Historical Research Center, our son Reese found some information on our family. The Dutch family name "van den Berge" is of a habitation name origin referring to a man "of/from the hill." The word *berg* in Dutch means *mountain*, or, obviously, *hill*, referring to a small mountain since there are really no mountains at all in Holland. Sometimes it is written as "Van den Berg" or as "van den Berghe."

The earliest reference found thus far is of a man named "Jacob van den Berghe" who was a "*Schepen*" (Ships) Magistrate in Amsterdam in 1365. It is believed that the first use of hereditary surnames in the Netherlands and Belgium dates from the thirteenth century in the regions of Flanders and Brabant. This usage spread to Amsterdam by the sixteenth century, and one notable bearer of the surname was the artist and curator "Simon van den Berg" (1812-1891). In 1880, he was named as the director of the Royal Museum in the Hague. The name "van den Berg" was introduced to the United States as early as 1847, in which year there is a record of the emigration of "Cornelius Vandenberg," who had sailed to New York on board the Dutch ship, the *Maasstroom*.

It is interesting that two of my uncles, my father's oldest brother, was named "Cornelius van den Berge" and the younger "Jacob van den Berge." In Holland, we call our own parents Pa and Moe, and the grandparents were called Opa and Oma or Opa and Opoe. My paternal grandfather, Opa Marinus van den Berge, was born on November 2, 1856, in the province of Zeeland in Holland in a small village named Ellemeet, with about 200 inhabitants. Opa's parents were members of the *Hervormde Kerk* (Reformed Church) and had gone through life with great difficulty. His father was a farm laborer, and the social circumstances were pitiful. In the wintertime, there was no work, so no money could be earned. Each year there was a big struggle to get through the winter.

One cold, rough winter in Ellemeet, the family circumstances were very bleak. Opa told his mother that there was an ice-skating race outside and beyond the village. The winner would receive a seventy-pound bag of potatoes. He said he was going to win the race for her. It was a long, tough race, but he won. At the finish line, there was a pole for the winner's hands to touch. He grabbed the pole and spun around it about ten times before he came to a stop. He received the prize and carried the seventy-pound bag of potatoes upon his shoulders and gave it to his mother. This reminds Linda of "Hans Brinker and the Silver Skates," a book, a movie, and a high school play she saw years ago.

As my father told us, when Opa turned eighteen, he was tired of the meager existence in Ellemeet and decided to immigrate to Rotterdam on a sailboat. This was quite an undertaking for him. It took the ship three days to make the journey. In the spring of 1874, he stepped ashore in Rotterdam at the East Square (*Oostplein*). Pa told us that Opa was a handsome man, big and strongly built. He was also determined and was able to make decisions quickly.

His first job in Rotterdam, at a syrup factory, illustrates this fact. According to Pa, a particular incident occurred prior to Opa becoming a Christian. Opa was ordered to work more hours without additional compensation. When Opa confronted his boss, he was told, "No one here is being paid for extra hours." They were arguing, standing next to a large vat of syrup and after a while Opa just picked up his boss and placed him in the vat. The syrup was up to his neck. Opa never found out how he got out.

Next, Opa found work in the polders (drained land surrounded by dikes) near Haarlem. At that time, around 1880, large draining projects were being carried out there. The working hours were from 7:00 a.m. to 7:00 p.m., and the wages were nine guilders (about $2.30) per week. On Saturdays, they also worked until 7:00 p.m.

A notable incident occurred in the polder where there was an inn. The innkeeper had a beautiful daughter. Every man fell for her, but all had been turned away when they tried to date her. Opa laughed at them and said he'd try to date her. One Saturday evening, he went to the inn and asked the daughter if she'd go out with him. She said yes. Outside, a good number of the men were waiting to see the result of this attempt. Suddenly, the door opened, and the couple came out, the daughter at Opa's arm. The men were surprised, and Opa pretended he didn't see them; but he was the hero of the day. He did not care for the girl, but he enjoyed the victory.

Later, Opa went back to Rotterdam and found a few odd jobs but soon found a good position as a woodcutter with the city of Rotterdam. His boss was a Mr. Pieter van Dijk, who also happened to be a deacon at the *Gereformeerde Gemeente Kerk* in Rotterdam. Mr. van Dijk took Opa under his wing, teaching him the work that was to be done, but also witnessed to him about God and his church. Opa had no interest in religion at that time and was turned off by it.

Opa met Johanna Wilhelmina van Beekum, who lived in Voorschoten in South Holland. He liked her, and they were soon married. After Opa was married for a while, an interesting thing happened. He came home one day to find out that his wife had bought a beautiful mirror. He asked her where she had bought it and why. She said that her mother thought they needed it and that it would look very good on one of the walls in their home. Apparently, this was not the first time her mother had advised her to purchase something. Opa thought he should put a stop to that. He took the mirror, went to the back patio, and slammed it down on the concrete into a million pieces. Then he looked his wife in the eye and said, "You did not marry your mother. You married me. From now on, any decisions about purchasing anything are made by you and me, no one else." That straightened that situation out very effectively. There were no more problems like that again.

Opa was not a religious man until one day he attended a church service in Rotterdam. When he was close to thirty years old, he had been invited a few times by a friend and finally decided to go. The story goes that in Ellemeet, years before, when he was about eighteen, he would go with some friends and "visit" a couple of churches on Sunday mornings. They would throw open a church's front door and actually throw rocks inside to scare the parishioners and the minister. This time, it was quite different.

As Pa tells it, when Opa was in this church in Rotterdam, he was overcome by the presence of God and gladly surrendered himself to the one who would be his Redeemer and his Savior. Opa has been quoted as saying, "That minister spoke right to me!" His path would not always be rosy, but God had assured him that his life would be in God's hands. After that, God seemed to use Opa as a target for revealing the Holy Spirit in him and through him in some unusual ways. He had become a totally different man.

Opa van den Berge

FAMILY, FAITH, AND MIRACLES

My niece, Johanna van den Berge, managed to send me a rare book called *Zijn Vuur En Haardstede*, written by J. Mastenbroek, part 2, 1914–1994, published in 1998. The book is about the church history of the *Gereformeerde Gemeente* church in Rotterdam. Opa van den Berge's contributions and church service are described on pages 159–161, but he is also mentioned in various other places in the book. The title of the book can be translated as *Fire and Hearth* or *Flame and Home*. Opa joined the church where Mr. van Dijk, his boss, was a deacon, and it wasn't long before Opa was elected to church deacon as well. He fulfilled his duties in that office for forty years with love and cheerfulness. He was a blessing to many.

Some wonderful things happened through Opa. Pa told us that when Opa took us up in prayer, we felt immediately at ease. At age nineteen, Toos, Pa's sister, was so ill that her doctors told her she only had a very short time to live. (Toos had become a Christian at a very early age.) When the doctor said this, Opa was driven to the Lord.

He later told Pa that he prayed until early morning and had begged God to save his daughter's life. Then the Lord revealed to him that his daughter would not die. Opa's thoughts were guided by the incident of Jesus changing water into wine at Cana during a wedding. He took up a glass of water and said to Toos, "Drink this. The Lord is powerful. He will perform a miracle on you."

She drank, and in the morning, she was completely healed. The physician was amazed. Opa said he went to the upper physician and told him God had performed a miracle. The doctor said, "That must be, because for me she was written up for dead."

I have very fond memories of Aunt Toos. I would visit her for a week during several summers in Delft when I was about twelve years old. I had a great time. She was a precious, sweet, Christian lady.

At age four, Pa was run over by a heavy vegetable wagon in front of the family's house. The neighbors picked him up and carried him inside. His abdomen was extensively injured. There was blood in his urine. Opa took him on his lap and called on the Lord in prayer. Opa wept. After an hour, he told his wife that their child could stand up again. Pa did and was completely better.

When Pa was eighteen, he had a serious lung infection. At the height of the disease crisis, as Pa told us, he was unconscious for three days and, of course, was very weak. That time as well, the Lord heard the prayer of Opa. Pa was healed very soon thereafter.

Another truly miraculous incident occurred later when Pa was engaged to be married to my mother around 1924. She developed a leg problem. It was either gangrene or cancer. Her leg was twice as thick as usual and black and green. She had seen a few doctors, but nothing could be done. Pa went to his father, Opa van den Berge, and asked him if he would pray for her. Moe's leg was to be amputated below the knee the next morning. Well, Opa prayed for her all night. In the morning, the nurse came to Moe's room to prepare her leg for surgery. She uncovered her leg and said, "I'm sorry. I guess it's the other leg!" She uncovered the other leg, and it was normal too. What a shock. The nurse told the doctors. They came running. They checked her armband to make sure she was the right patient and asked Moe what happened. She could not answer. She just cried from happiness. The doctors were stunned. Moe has had two healthy legs since then for the rest of her life, until she died from other causes when she was seventy-seven.

When Pa was two and a half years old, in 1903, his mother died after being ill for several days. Unfortunately, he never really knew her. She passed away joyful in her faith that Christ had died for her also at the cross on Golgotha. Her deathbed was, for all, a sermon that we must be united with God.

Opa married again, and Pa spoke very highly of his second mother. He said that she deserves a place of honor in our hearts. She was a quiet Christian, had a serving character, and meant so much to the family. She, too, died later, fully believing that she would live eternally with the Lord. Pa and his brother-in-law, Abram van Bochove, spent all night with her at her deathbed. Those were very special moments never to be forgotten.

Pa had married Moe, and she was from a wonderful Christian family. Her father, Mr. Jan Bakker, who to us was "Opa" Bakker, was born on November 6, 1867, at Zwijndrecht. He was a resolute, hard-working man who did everything to maintain a good life for his family. He too experienced the hand of God.

Opa Bakker

Opa Bakker's wife, Opoe Bakker, had an operation, and there was a large hospital bill to be paid, too large for Opa's wallet. At the doctor's office, he was told that the whole bill had been paid. Pa told us that on the way to the doctor's office, the Lord gave Opa Bakker these words to feel in his heart: "I forgave you all that debt," (Matthew 18:32b).

On another occasion, Opoe Bakker had to go to the hospital for a major operation. After she recovered, again there was a big bill to be paid and no money to pay it. One Saturday, Opa Bakker received notice to see the doctor. As he arrived, not knowing what the visit was about, he suspected that the doctor wanted to talk about the bill. But the doctor was very pleasant and asked how Mrs. Bakker was doing. As Opa Bakker was about to leave, he asked, "Doctor, how about the bill?"

"Oh, don't you know? That's all been taken care of. It's all paid."

Opa never found out who paid it. God is good.

Mother (Opoe) Bakker was also a quiet servant and a wonderful Christian. She died on June 25, 1923. She and Opa Bakker had two sons and five daughters. One of their daughters died of typhus at age fourteen. She was a lovely girl who was converted to God at a young age. Interestingly, Opa van den Berge led the funeral. Opa Bakker remarried later.

Pa encouraged us to realize that the most important thing we need to do is to walk with the Lord daily. The Lord promised Opa van den Berge once, "I shall be a God for you, but also for your seed," (Genesis 17:7b). He said, "The fear of the Lord is the beginning of wisdom," (Proverbs 9:10a). Nothing is as important as the assurance that one spends his or her life with God. Pa said, "May God give you something of that great good that never perishes but remains into eternity." Amen.

For a few years after the war, my uncles on Pa's side (their parents were deceased by then) would all visit their older brother, Cornelius, at his house. It was intended as sort of a "keeping the family together" type of meeting. Then, for a few years, the brothers would visit one another on their birthdays. It was great fun for all of us. They would share war stories over coffee and pastries (*gebakjes*).

There was much to be thankful for. In spite of all the dangers, not one from any of our families was killed during the war. That was simply amazing. The only exception that might be noted is that Opa Bakker, Moe's father, died of a major heart attack on his way to church one very cold Sunday morning on February 20, 1944, during the last months of the war. He collapsed on a street, and the people who lived there took him in; but he had already gone to his heavenly Father.

He was an amazing man too. He had worked for a rice company

for many years before retiring. Collecting his retirement pension, he had to walk a few kilometers to the rice company owner's house each Saturday morning to pick up the money. It was not long before the owner said one Saturday, "I am sorry, Mr. Bakker, but this is the last payment I can give you. There is no need to come again." Well, Opa Bakker was shocked, but he persevered and decided to start a business selling grains, nuts, seeds, and the like.

He bought a couple of wagons with a bicycle set-up in the back of each, so one could sit and peddle the wagon. People who were moving or needed some sort of cargo transportation could rent a wagon from Opa. The business did very well; and he and his wife, Opoe Bakker, survived and were even able to leave an inheritance for their children.

I recall visiting Opa Bakker on the Disselstraat in South Rotterdam. He was very nice and pleasant to talk to. He even kicked a soccer ball with me while he was wearing wooden shoes. He was a devout Christian man who implicitly trusted the Lord. He was also a deacon in his church.

Years earlier, when Moe still lived with Opa Bakker on the Hoogeboomstraat in Zuid (South) Rotterdam, there was one Christmas when there was practically no food at all. They were pretty poor. On that Christmas Eve, Opa prayed and trusted the Lord that there would be food for his family. In the evening, the doorbell rang, and a man said, "Is this the Bakker house?" When Opa Bakker said that it was, the man deposited a basket filled with food on the bottom step and left without saying a word. They never found out who it was. God had supplied.

I must not forget to tell the circumstances in which Opa van den Berge died. One day, at age seventy-six, he called my father in and asked him to take some notes. (This was also described in the book *Zijn Vuur En Haardstede*, on page 160.) My father was the most administrative-type person in the family. Opa began dictating his own funeral. Pa asked him, "What are you doing?" Opa told him that he would need this very soon. So he resumed dictating the arrangements of his own funeral. It was to be a very simple funeral, nothing fancy. He was a very humble man. He also told Pa who was to be invited and who was not to be invited.

Well, six days later, Opa was tired and decided to rest in bed for a while. He had asked his wife day or so earlier to purchase a new shirt and undershirt for his funeral. Opa was resting on his bed while my grandmother was fixing his lunch. Then Opa prayed, sang a hymn, said amen, and he was home. He had known he was going to die very soon. The Lord had told him.

MY NEW AMERICAN FAMILY

I have been so blessed to have come from two Christian families and to have married into another Christian family. Linda's parents both came from Christian families. Please do not think I am bragging about this. I am just blessed things have worked out this way. Linda's father, Mr. Griffith Byrd Dorn, was a remarkable man. He was a very hard worker.

He graduated with honors from Clemson University in June 1933, majoring in textile chemistry. As mentioned before, he left South Carolina and visited Frostburg, Maryland, where he found his wife-to-be, Eira. He had become a route salesman for the Jewel Tea Company. One of his regular customers was the Rev. William David Reese family and Eira was their daughter whom he married soon after they met.

When World War II began, he and his family of five were living in Greensboro, North Carolina, where he continued working as a manager for the Jewel Tea Company. In 1940, World War II broke out, and his commission with the army had expired. During his college years, he had been a member of the Army National Guard and ROTC. So he enlisted in the US Naval Reserve in December of 1943.

Dad then temporarily moved his family to Frostburg, Maryland, where they stayed with Reverend and Mrs. Reese while he received training in Princeton, New Jersey, at the naval officer training school. He graduated from chemical warfare school as a lieutenant (junior grade) in the navy and was subsequently assigned as director of training with the naval district at Camp Elliott in San Diego, California. He, with his wife and three children in tow, drove his family across the country over a two-week period or more, driving on famed Route 66, the route made famous in the song "Get Your Kicks on Route 66." Linda remembers, at age six or seven, seeing the fun "Burma-Shave" sayings on the roadside signs. Despite a few bouts with carsickness, it was an unforgettable adventure for Linda, Griff, and David.

Housing in San Diego was scarce, but through the help of a Baptist church, they temporarily lived in a lovely home, owned by a wonderful, elderly gentleman named Mr. Wood. These were difficult times for the young Dorn family, but they adjusted. Linda's dad (I'll refer to him as Dad) organized an officers' chemical warfare instructors' school, and he taught officers on the navy ships on the West Coast. Had chemicals been used in wartime, Dad would have had to go to the war front.

The children, on the other hand, were enjoying a wonderful adventure. Soon, Linda's family moved to a more suitable home in San Diego, in walking distance from the school. To Linda, who was seven, school was easy and fun. She enjoyed the "south of the border" influence and music. The house they had moved into was next to a canyon. She saw wildflowers she had never seen before, learned to enjoy avocadoes, and found the weather to be ideal.

When Dad was released from the service after the war as a Lt. U.S.N.R., Lieutenant United States Naval Reserve. the family left for Baltimore, Maryland, where his job with Jewel Companies, Inc. awaited him. Dad stayed with the company and climbed up in the ranks, finally retiring in 1972 as the eastern regional manager and vice president. He was offered the presidency, but he declined, preferring rather to retire and spend more time with his family.

Linda's paternal grandfather, Mr. Thomas E. Dorn, was born in the Callison community of Greenwood County in South Carolina. He was the son of George E. and Elizabeth Byrd Dorn, members of families identified with the life and development of that part of South Carolina dating from the colonial days. Mr. Dorn attended Furman and Mercer and received his diploma from the old South Carolina coeducational institute at Edgefield.

He first taught in Saluda County, where he established the Zoar High School. Returning to Greenwood, he taught school in Greenwood County; and in 1917, he was elected superintendent of education, holding this office for sixteen years. In his younger years, before his marriage, he was a circuit preacher. He would travel with a Bible and a shotgun and preach in various locations as far as Chicago. (I cannot imagine riding horseback from South Carolina to Chicago!)

He was active in the First Baptist Church of Greenwood. In 1905, he married Pearl Griffith of Saluda. They had ten children. Mrs. Dorn was honored by the general assembly and the governor of South Carolina for having seven sons in the service at the same time. The photos below are a courtesy of *The Index Journal of Greenwood, South Carolina*, July 21, 2005 issue, which featured an article, titled, "7 Brothers For America," which highlighted Mr. Watson Dorn, who described his and his brothers' actions as volunteers in the military during World War II[4].

The Dorn brothers from left to right: Thomas, Griffith, George, Jackson, Watson, Bryan, and Charles.

I am very grateful to them and many others like them for having brought me and many others freedom from tyranny. God brought me into a family of freedom fighters in the United States. They were active in different areas of World War II. Uncle Tom served in the US Air Force; Griffith (Dad) was in the navy, as mentioned before; and

Uncle George was an army flight instructor. Uncle Jackson served in the US Army in the Italian campaign, and Uncle Watson served in the navy as a communications officer on a US Naval vessel in the Pacific.

Uncle Bryan, who was named after a great orator, William Jennings Bryan (hence, his name was William Jennings Bryan Dorn), was a great speaker and storyteller in his own right. He served in General Patton's Army, Third Division, and fought in the Battle of the Bulge in Europe. Uncle Charles was a navy pilot and a heavyweight-boxing champion in his unit. I also understand that he was an excellent navigator, who was able to drop some well-placed bombs on the enemy.

Uncle Bryan eventually became a US congressman from South Carolina and served as such in Washington, DC, for over twenty-six years with distinction. In August 2005 he died at age eighty-nine at the Barrett House, his home, in Greenwood, South Carolina. This is quite a resume of seven brothers willing to risk their lives to protect the homeland and bring freedom to other people in the process. This, to me, is like a miniature picture of World War II: freedom fighters willing to right wrongs at great risk because the cause is so great. They were the total opposite of the suicide bombers, terrorists, and other tyrants of today.

God was on the side of the freedom fighters, who bring healing, freedom, and restoration to people they don't even personally know. War is a very dirty business, but these fighters were not afraid to get their hands dirty for me. This reminds me of the Bible verse that says, "Greater love has no one than this, that a man lay down his life for his friends," (John 15:13). Now, I know that some would say that the United States went to war in self-defense—which was one of the reasons, I'm sure. But in the process, so much good was done for so many innocent people who suffered greatly.

Linda's maternal grandparents were wonderful people, very nice and hardworking emigrants from Wales. Theirs is also a fascinating story. Reverend Reese, Linda's grandfather, came from Craig-Cein-Parc, Swansea, South Wales. He was a son of David (Dafydd) and Miriam Rees. Mr. Dafydd Rees was originally from Cilybebyll,

Wales. He died in 1884 at the young age of thirty-one. Rev. Reese was educated at the Old Carmathan School, Ammanfoyd Academy, and the University of Wales, Cardiff, where he studied theology. After graduation, he accepted the pastorate of St. David's Church at Pembrokeshire in Wales and served as pastor there for seven and one half years. Rev. Reese married Winifred Thomas. They eventually settled in the United States in 1912.

Mrs. Reese was a native of Pembrokeshire. In America, Rev. Reese became the pastor of a Baptist Church in Taylor, Pennsylvania, for five and one-half years before becoming the pastor of the Mt. Zion Welsh Memorial Baptist Church in Frostburg, Maryland, where he served for over thirty years. During those years, Linda's mother, Eira, was born in Taylor, Pennsylvania (Eira means snow; it was snowing when she was born), and Richard Blethyn and his sister, Bronwen, were born in Frostburg. He accomplished a remarkable record of service to his congregation, and he served on a number of boards and various community groups. One very cold winter Sunday, although he was recovering from the flu, he kept his commitment to speak at another church in Frostburg. Mrs. Reese urged him not to go. While preaching the sermon, he fainted and passed away.

A nephew of Mrs. Reese, Richard D.V. Llewellyn Lloyd, a.k.a. Richard Llewellyn, wrote the novel *How Green Was My Valley*, in 1940, which was made into an Oscar-winning motion picture with Walter Pidgeon and Maureen O'Hara. The story actually takes place around St. David's, a coal-mining town in Wales. Mr. Lloyd was very familiar with the Reese family, as he lived in the area. Mrs. Reese and Richard grew up together. The movie features Rev. Reese's family in various ways. Walter Pidgeon portrayed Rev. Reese as "Mr. Griffith." Maureen O'Hara portrayed Winifred Thomas (later Mrs. Reese).

When, in 1959, I went to ask Dad if I could marry Linda, I expected a negative response because I was really not prepared. I had just gotten "off the boat" as it were, had almost no money, and had only a high school equivalency diploma. I had a long way to go if I hoped to become a dentist. However, I suppose he had looked me over and decided to take a chance on me. He also knew that Linda and I were head over heels in love with each other and, I guess, sensed that we were meant for each other. So he gave his approval, and I was delighted and felt quite honored. He was a solid family man. He and Mom were a wonderful couple and a perfect example to all of us. They loved each other very much and, to the end, were totally loyal to each other. Dad was ninety-two when he died in 2003.

Pa and Moe got along very well with Dad and Mom. When they first met, Linda's parents took Pa and Moe and us out for dinner. We met them at their home. Once inside, Linda's mother came down the steps, and she looked gorgeous. She was wearing a new dress, but somehow Dad did not notice that. So Mom said, "Well, Griff, did you notice my new dress?" upon which Dad answered very quickly, "Oh, honey, I was admiring your beautiful face so much that I didn't notice the dress!" Pa thought that was a great answer and got the biggest kick out of that. This was a great start to a wonderful relationship between Linda's parents and mine.

From left to right: Moe, Linda, Mom, Nancy (Linda's sister), Dad, John (eyes closed), and Pa located at a Washington, DC, restaurant

---

Mom was quite a lady. Just after Thanksgiving in 2007, she went to her reward in heaven at age ninety-three. Dad and Mom were survived by four children, thirteen grandchildren, and twenty-one great-grandchildren. As the Bible says, "Children are a heritage from the Lord," (Psalm 127:3) and, "Happy is the man who has his quiver full of them," (Psalm 127:5). We think they did extremely well.

Mom was quite a lady!

Around Christmas, when the family got together, with all the grandchildren, it was wonderful to see that big crowd of people getting along so well honoring their parents and grandparents. To be part of a fine Christian family in the United States today—a country that promotes and tries to export freedom to other parts of the world, the kind of freedom my family in Holland did without for five years—is just a privileged thing to experience.

SMOKING DISCONTINUED

I had quit smoking cigarettes around the time I entered dental school. Linda doesn't remember seeing me smoke any cigarettes. Around 1960, smoking was popular. My father had smoked since the war began. It had become a nervous habit with him. I remember that when I came home from a trip across the ocean, I usually brought Pa a couple of cartons of cigarettes, such as Lucky Strikes or Camels, as I mentioned earlier. He seemed to really appreciate that. I smoked when I was in the military and in the merchant marines, although I was never a heavy smoker. When I was studying extensively in school, I did smoke some small cigars; but Linda really didn't like the smell of cigars, so I switched to smoking a pipe. During long, seemingly boring hours of studying, smoking a pipe seemed to take the edge off. It was relaxing. Linda found the cherry pipe tobacco odor more acceptable and perhaps even pleasant because her grandfather, Rev. Reese, smoked a pipe before or after his work sometimes and it rather intrigued her. She recalls one time watching him fill, tamp, and light that pipe and sit back in his favorite chair as he listened to the Pittsburgh Pirates ballgame on the radio, smoking the pipe contentedly, the pleasant-smelling smoke wafting in the air.

As I came to the end of the dental school experience, I recall getting a little tired of all the things you had to do to light the pipe. You had to take it apart, clean it, put it back together, put the cleaning equipment away again, and then stuff the pipe tobacco into the head of the pipe, pack it tight, and light it. Then, if you did not keep smoking it, it would quickly go out and you had to light it again. Finally, I came to the conclusion that I didn't really need to do all this, and I decided to quit altogether.

Right after graduation, I attended a dental convention in Baltimore; and there was a booth that offered a free lung capacity test. This measures the lung's maximum capacity to take in and blow out air. I remember vividly that I could breathe out two liters of air when I exhaled the maximum amount of air in one breath. Then, five years later, I was again at a dental convention, this time in Houston, Texas, where I repeated the same test. I had completely quit my smoking habit right after the last lung capacity test five years earlier. This time, I could exhale three liters of air, a fifty percent improvement in my lung capacity. What an amazing difference. This totally convinced me that smoking was not a good thing.

The other piece of evidence against smoking I acquired was during my dental anesthesiology training in Pittsburgh, when I was assisting in the operating room. I saw patients' lungs when their chests were opened up for any kind of heart or lung surgery. Normally, a healthy lung is pink in color, sort of like a pink sponge, but some of the lungs of heavy smokers, mineworkers, and steelworkers, as well as those who had lived in Pittsburgh for many years, had gray lungs with irregular patches of light and dark gray. The air in Pittsburgh in 1967–1968, while we lived there, was not very clean.

I recall that John G.'s and Reese's knees were dirty black when they first played on the back porch of our upstairs apartment in the afternoon, the day after we had arrived, even though Linda had cleaned the porch in the morning, and it was a covered porch! There was a lot of soot in the air from the steel factories. When I looked out of the sixth-story window from the hospital where I worked, I could see just a heavy cloud of smoke from the steel factories over the city every morning. I understand that the situation in Pittsburgh is much better now as far as the cleanliness of the air is concerned.

FAMILY LIFE IN ELLICOTT CITY

Our first two sons were born prior to graduation, while I was still in dental school in 1964 and 1966. Our first son, John Griffith, was born in June. Linda was doing fine until there was a false alarm. We went to Women's Hospital in Baltimore and were sent back home. Linda had also developed back pain. A couple of days later, the back pain became very severe. I called the hospital and told them we were coming in.

I carried Linda into the car and rushed her to the hospital; with the lights on and blowing the horn at times, I drove as fast as I could. When I arrived, I got out of the car and knocked on the entrance door, which was locked. A voice came out of the wall, asking, "Who are you?" And when I told them who I was, the voice said, "Do you have insurance?" I responded, "You better open this door right now! I called to tell you I was coming. My wife is in a lot of pain!"

I went back to the car, picked Linda up, and carried her to the entrance. Finally the door opened, and an aid scurried to get a wheelchair for her. What an experience. And poor Linda was in such pain. The doctor's diagnosis: "Every woman who goes through delivery has some back pain." Well, when Linda delivered a boy, our first of four sons, John Griffith, it was a welcome and happy event. But she still had back pains. She was dismissed a couple of days later, and I took her home. The next day, because her pain was growing in severity, I took Linda to St. Agnes Hospital Emergency Room. It turns out she had a kidney infection!

We really wanted my parents to be there when the baby was delivered, so we talked Pa and Moe into coming and staying in the United States indefinitely. Moe studied English in preparation for their arrival. Both Pa and Moe were very excited and really looking forward to it. They did arrive in June of 1964, just before John G. was born. My brothers, Martin and Jack, came over eventually and were married in the United States too. Having lived in Holland, their homeland, for some sixty-four years, with still so many family and cultural ties, it was quite a decision for my parents to come to live in the United States. It took a lot of courage. They lived with us for awhile before moving into an apartment in Columbia, Maryland.

In June of 1966, our second son, William David Reese, who goes by Reese, was born at Union Memorial Hospital. Fortunately, his arrival was less traumatic for Linda than her first delivery. He came into the world very calmly. Our third son, Martin (Marty), was also born at Union Memorial Hospital in Baltimore in 1972, during hurricane Agnes. His delivery was also normal. During delivery, I was sitting next to the anesthesiologist when Linda said, just prior to the big moment, "I wonder if it's going to be a boy or a girl." The anesthesiologist said, "Probably."

Alan Thomas (Al) was born in 1975 at St. Agnes Hospital by way of caesarean section. After his birth, Linda remained in the hospital for nine days. All four babies were beautiful, of course—or, rather, handsome. But all were quite healthy gifts from God.

In 1976 we bought a house in Ellicott City, in neighboring Howard County, not far from Arbutus, where I had started a dental practice. In Arbutus we lived in a row house, and the house in Ellicott City was bigger. From here we made lots of excursions into the surrounding areas.

When Moe lived in her apartment on Plum Tree Drive in Ellicott City for a time, she kept quite busy. Since she was such an excellent seamstress, she began doing some clothing alterations for friends as a favor. Some insisted on paying her something for the wonderful work she did. Word spread, and this became a new business venture for her.

My mother was a saint. She appreciated everything in the United States, and she loved people. She had an adventurous spirit as well. She once went on a long trip by herself. She bought a bus ticket to go by Greyhound around the country to Chicago, Los Angeles, Houston, Oklahoma, and then back to Ellicott City. She either had friends or made friends wherever she went. In Tulsa, she visited a friend; and in Los Angeles, she visited with her niece, Lenie, from Holland, who had moved west.

Another wonderful aspect of Moe's life in Maryland was that she got along so well with her daughters-in-law. Linda and Moe were like Ruth and Naomi from the Bible story. After Pa died, Moe lived with us for over a year in Ellicott City. She went with us to the beach in Ocean City and to Disney World in Florida and went with us on other trips too. She was always great company. There have been no mother-in-law problems in our family, on either side. During the last few months of her life, she became weaker and then rather ill with congestive heart failure, unfortunately. She needed oxygen and other help while at our house and felt very bad that she could not do more.

One day, she told Linda that she thought she was too much trouble for her; but Linda reassured her that she was not and that she felt toward her as Ruth must have felt toward Naomi in the Bible. They wept and hugged each other—a very touching moment Linda will never forget.

Moe also got along very well with our boys. She would play games with them, and all had lots of fun. We would all get together with her after church on Sunday when she still lived in her apartment. Moe had coffee and delicious goodies ready. The atmosphere was what we call in Dutch, "*gezellig*." There is really no accurate translation for that word except to describe it as "cozy, intimate, very touching, and pleasant to be in each other's company—a warm atmosphere." It was a bonding environment where we'd get to know each other a little better each time. It reminded me of the bonding we experienced in Holland during the war when we were huddled together in a small apartment for many hours.

SOCCER

As a young boy, I played a good deal of soccer in Holland, as that was, and still is, the national sport. I played on an amateur team in Delft, called CSVD (Christian Sports Organization of Delft), so I taught our four sons how to play the game in Ellicott City in the back yard. We had a large backyard in Ellicott City which was perfect to get in a good soccer game. The property was about one acre in size, mostly a grassy open space with a pond at the bottom of the yard. Friends would come over, and we enjoyed the camaraderie while playing soccer or sometimes softball with the ladies too.

During the winter, we improvised the game downstairs in the basement. We had an unfinished basement with a concrete floor, which we painted green to make it look like a soccer field. We used a soft soccer ball from Toys R Us that was small, not too hard, and did not bounce, but it rolled very well. The area was not that big, perhaps forty by forty feet square with a pole in the middle. We played two against two, of course; and as Alan grew older, he became a goalkeeper and did very well, even at four to six years old. We had made up a couple of small wooden goals, so it was not so easy to score. We found out that this was great exercise because ten or fifteen minutes into the game, we were all perspiring; and half an hour later, our shirts were all wet.

One day, my nephew, Renee, came over to the house to visit; and after a while, on that Sunday afternoon, we invited him to play downstairs. He is a big man who played a lot of soccer in Holland and is quite adept on his feet. So he laughed and said, "What do you mean? Playing in a basement with a little soft kiddie ball? Me?"

"Well, just come and see," we said. He sized up the situation and joined us, and soon he was perspiring, enjoying the finesse of the game we played. He played afterward with us many times, and it became a popular outlet for all of us men to get some exercise and have fun during the winter.

JACK

My youngest brother, Jack, lives with his wife, Lee, in Manassas, Virginia. They were also at Martin's seventy-fifth birthday party in 2004, when Martin came to visit from Holland; and we had a really nice reunion. I am so thankful to have two wonderful brothers who helped me recall specific events from the war. Jack (Joop) has three fine daughters: Jennifer, Laura, and Susan. Jack's first wife, Carol, lives near us with her mother, Mrs. Evelyn Rae, in Ellicott City; and we are great friends with all of them. We all get along really well and enjoy seeing each other from time to time.

PART III

WHO WINS?

CHAPTER 14
WORLDVIEW

God is in charge of our lives, whether we like to admit it or not. God refers to Israel as the "Apple of His eye" (Zechariah 2:8). This is tantamount to saying that if anyone goes against Israel, one goes against God, whether it is an individual or a country. God looks for those who seek him, those who love righteousness and goodness, and for those who love their neighbors as themselves. He does things his way; and we'd better adjust to that or pay the consequences. The sooner any individual or any country does things God's way, the better off they'll all be.

The Hitlers of this world have tried it their way. It does not work. The reason the United States has been successful thus far is that we are a Christian nation—at least that is how we got started. If we keep falling away from the founding Christian principles, we'll have many more problems. The Bible says, "When the righteous are in authority, the people rejoice; but when a wicked man rules, the people groan" (Proverbs 29:2). (Many people groaned in World War II.)

The meaning of righteous is right standing with God, doing things His way. The "righteousness" of our nation helped defeat the unrighteousness of another. "Righteousness exalts a nation, but sin is a reproach to any people" (Proverbs 14:34). When a man pleases God, some things can happen that may not be very obvious. "When a man's ways please the Lord, He makes even his enemies to be at peace with him" (Proverbs 16: 7). (My father certainly showed that with the Nazis.) For one, there will be some protection. Billy Graham has said each Christian has at least two angels who are there to minister to and protect the individual. Then there is God's guiding hand, doing things we often do not even notice. These things are available to anyone who wants them. In my daily walk, I try to be aware of God's presence and guidance as much as possible, although this is a challenge.

I want to go back over some instances in which I am pretty sure that the incidents were not just coincidences but God-incidences; that is, God's guiding hand doing things we don't often notice. This review will not be exhaustive, just a few highlights. I also believe this applies to most people if they really think about it and are inclined toward God.

When my father escaped from the bombardment in Rotterdam while buildings around him were destroyed and many perished, it would be safe for me to say that God protected my father. Now let me immediately emphasize something here. This is not to say or imply that my father or any of us were better or more holy or more righteous than anyone else. Why did many die while my father and others did not? Only God has the answer for that. Many people prayed during the war, and a lot died anyway.

Corrie Ten Boom prayed, and her family prayed. Corrie somehow survived, and some of her family did not. Were her prayers better? I doubt that very much. When we get to heaven, we can ask God about that. We do know that he certainly showed his plan and purpose, indeed through her, to be his witness after the war. Many others were blessed by knowing and hearing this particularly godly woman.

Our apartment in Rotterdam was spared from any bombings during the first few days of the war and all the rest of the five years as well. God protected us and many others. Dr. Ernest Cassutto and his family survived the war. He was a wonderful Jewish man who believed that Jesus was his Messiah and that God protected him. I'm sure, because, like Corrie ten Boom, God had a mission for him and his family to fulfill. As we know, many Jews and Christians did die.

Did God protect Arend Segaar and his Underground friends when they overpowered the Nazi truck driver and his Nazi friend and went into the Rotterdam jail and freed their Underground friends? Probably.

Was Martin supernaturally protected when he could not ride on the Citroen with the Nazi officers and when he was almost arrested when four Nazis had been hanged in Garderen? I would think so. I think God protected Martin during the whole trip to his Uncle Piet in Garderen because of the prayers of his parents.

When Uncle Jacob was sent back to Holland so quickly after he had to go to Germany, one had to wonder about the effects of prayer by family and relatives.

Remember when the razzias were held and Pa and Rien missed the cutoff on both sides? They were fifteen and forty-four. Those between seventeen and forty-two had to go to Germany.

I believe it was God who put the vision in my head and heart of seeing the United States after the war. The way things worked out, I could not have planned it all myself.

Did God protect me when I worked for the furrier in Rotterdam and was driving that motorized fur coat carrier, about to plow into the car in front of me when that car moved at just the right time and the right speed so I would not hit it? I think so. He has rescued me from so many scrapes and potential disasters.

I think a very big one was when, on the first day on the New Amsterdam, the older sailor offered me a beer and the glass fell out of my hand. The dropping of a glass from my hand never happened before or since. I firmly believe that God rescued me from alcoholism right there. I have never had the desire to drink alcohol since. (I drank a rum and cola in Havana because I was thirsty and naive about any after-effects. Today, I occasionally drink a glass of wine.)

I firmly believe God was with Pa throughout all of his activities, especially at his office with the Nazi physicians, where he interpreted and saved quite a few of his countrymen from exportation to Germany. I believe God was with the Catholic priest who hid a radio and received BBC news daily, which he shared with Pa many times. Also, when the priest, Pa and Uncle Cornelius hid Jewish people during the war, God protected them all, I firmly believe.

When allies, mainly Americans, brought the Dutch freedom on May 5, 1945, God was with all of them. It was a great victory over Satan and all his evil demons.

The fact that we did not starve to death in spite of massive shortages or contract any major disease is a miracle. So often, a little bit of food came just in the nick of time, as in the instance of the sugar beet.

Then we recall how, on Christmas Eve, a basket of food was delivered to Opa Bakker's house and how the hospital bill was suddenly paid—by whom we never found out.

How about the way Opa Vandenberge passed away? He knew a few days in advance and was not sick. He just went to his prepared home in heaven after dictating his own funeral to Pa.

Of course, we can never forget that Moe's leg was healed so miraculously. One night she had a black and green, swollen leg that needed to be amputated; and the next morning, both of her legs were normal.

I cannot skip over the fact that I passed the high school equivalency test with so little education. I should not have passed it. God must have been with me. I know God was with me the way he had me meet Linwood in the middle of the ocean to get me to Baltimore in order to marry Linda. God guided me into situations so I could meet Captain Brackx and Captain Ruygrok, who helped me to stay in America. I have met many other people on my journey, and I shall not attempt to name them all. There are just too many, and I am bound to forget some.

I am convinced God puts people in our paths at critical times in all of our lives. God has a hand in all of this. The Bible says, "But the very hairs of your head are all numbered" (Matthew 10:30). Also, "For lo, He who forms the mountains, and creates the wind, and declares to man what is His thought…" (Amos 4:13). We do well to recognize that and that it is not "luck."

When someone asks, "What is your worldview?" What do you say? For most people, the answer to this question involves an explanation of what life around them is all about.

How did we get here, and where are we going? I believe in the

God of Abraham, Isaac, and Jacob, and I believe he created all of us. I also believe he is the Creator, owner, and ruler of the universe and that Jesus Christ is Lord of everything. The Word (Jesus Christ) was made flesh and dwelt among us physically and now spiritually. Jesus Christ arose from being dead and is alive now to save people from going to hell if they believe in him. The Father, Son, and Holy Spirit are one.[5]

What, then, is my relationship with him today? It is a love, dependence, trust, and a respectful relationship in that I believe what the Bible says, the Bible being the divinely inspired Word of God, and it has become my manual for living. The Bible supports this fact with many Bible verses, such as:

> For You formed my inward parts; You covered me in my mother's womb. I will praise You, for I am fearfully and wonderfully made; Marvelous are Your works, And that my soul knows very well.
>
> Psalm 139:13-14 (NKJV)

Daily Bible reading is a must for me even if it is only one chapter. I don't think anyone can be really finished studying the Bible. It is so deep with many aspects and layers of understanding. There is so much to learn about the presence of God in one's life and the power of God. My father used to say that there is a solution for every problem on earth in the Bible. More copies have been sold of the Bible than any other book in the world.

I have been blessed tremendously, and all the credit goes to God. Please consider this book as a personal letter to you, that you may enjoy this life through him and know that heaven is awaiting us.[6]

Now, one can ignore this way of thinking and not believe it, but that would be like not believing in gravity. Gravity is here, and so is God. God's existence is irrefutable because there is such overwhelming evidence of his presence among us. I also believe that God is bigger than one denomination. Linda and I have Lutheran, Methodist,

Jewish, Roman Catholic and many other friends. We pray for people of all denominations, including Muslims and we pray that they all will be kept out of hell and will go to heaven.

I hope my life story has encouraged you. Obviously, I am a Christian, and I hope you are too. If you are not, I want you to realize that God loves you and has a plan for your life. If your life were to end today, do you know what will happen to you? You can know.

You may think it is impossible because of your past. But with God, all things are possible; he is a forgiving God. Jesus Christ died for you, and he is the only Son of God who has been raised from the dead. When you accept the fact that he died for your sins and invite him into your heart, you will be saved from going to hell when you die. It's that simple. You must mean it, of course.

Once you have said that prayer, believing that Jesus Christ is God, asking him to forgive all your sins, inviting him into your life, you will have been born again and you will be saved; you will go to heaven when you die. The only alternative is to go to hell, which is very real; and God certainly does not want you to go there. It is a very, very horrible place—for eternity!

If you prayed this prayer, you need to tell someone. I suggest that you call someone at CBN (Christian Broadcasting Network): 1-800-759-0700 or TBN (Trinity Broadcasting Network): 1-888-731-1000 (both available 24/7) or a local clergyman who believes this way, and they will be very happy for you and encourage you. This is the most important prayer you will have prayed in all your life. I also encourage you to join a Bible-believing local church. I hope to meet you in heaven one day.

CHAPTER 15
A FINAL OBSERVATION

I want to share with you the following observation. You have read my story of switching countries, and you may ask, "What did he learn from the immigration experience?" Well, for many years, I have wondered why it is that, at times, millions of people are deceived and don't realize it until it is too late. Why did not millions of smart, intelligent, decent, and cultural German people discern what Hitler was up to?

Well, a friend just sent me a letter, written by Paul E. Marik for the Arutz Sheva E-mail News Service, describing a situation of a German aristocratic family prior to World War II. The man owned a number of industries and estates. "Very few Germans were true Nazis," he said, "but many enjoyed the return of German pride, and many were too busy to care. I was one of those who just thought that the Nazis were a bunch of fools. So the majority just sat back and let it happen. Then, before we knew, they owned us, and we had lost control and the end of the world had come. My family lost everything. I ended up in a concentration camp, and the Allies destroyed my factories. Many people have experienced similar tragedies throughout history.

"We are told again and again by 'experts' and 'talking heads,'" Marik continues, "that Islam is the religion of peace. Although this unqualified statement may be true, it is *entirely irrelevant.* This is a very important statement. The fact is that fanatics rule Islam at this moment in history. It is the fanatics who march, wage wars around the world, and slaughter Christians (and Jews). They also kill tribal groups throughout Africa and are gradually taking over the entire continent in an Islamic wave. It is the fanatics who bomb, behead, murder, and honor kill. It is the fanatics who take over many mosques and who teach their young to become suicide bombers. The peaceful majority is cowed and extraneous. They just 'let it happen.'"

It's important to understand that Russia and China were comprised of peaceful people, but the fanatic leaders killed one hundred twenty and seventy million of their own people respectively. So, also, peace-loving Germans, Japanese, Chinese, Rwandans, Serbs, Afghans, Iraqis, Palestinians, Somalis, Nigerians, Algerians, Cambodians, Vietnamese, and many others died because the peaceful majority did not speak up until it was too late. Sometimes these fanatics were even voted in legally, as in the case of Hitler. Perhaps even today, in the last US election, did we as voters do the right thing? Time will tell. It was Sir Edmund Burke who once said, "All that is necessary for evil to triumph is for good men to do nothing."

Sometimes I have a sinking feeling that, just as in the 1930s in Germany, we are drifting today into socialism, with banks being taken over, sub-prime mortgages being extended to unqualified buyers, as well as large companies succumbing to government control with the threat of all of us losing many freedoms. High unemployment and terrorist threats are prevalent now. Many people are saying, "What in the world is happening to our country?" Something is terribly wrong.

For me, it is obvious that socialism does not work, which is where our government seems to be headed. To me, socialism, with some elite liberals and progressives in charge as possible future fanatics, is one step away from communism. I certainly do not want to go from hell to heaven and then back again to hell/tyranny. I much prefer Mr. Reagan's policies of the '80s: lower taxes, smaller government, a strong defense, a sound foreign policy. I like promotion of free enterprise and relying on the providential hand that has protected us all along. We were respected around the world at that time. We must protect this nation's sovereignty.

Our founding fathers had it right. They respected God, our Creator, from whom we have received our rights; they didn't come from our government. I believe that America has been blessed because we are a Christian nation, honoring the Judeo-Christian ethic. If we kick God out of the classroom and the universities, we are bound to get in trouble. When Israel, or any other group or individual, disobeyed God, problems followed. History is full of evidence on that score.

This land is so great, with such tremendous opportunities to prosper, to be helpful in the community, and to serve others. The freedoms we have are awesome, and we must guard against anyone trying to take them away.

The freedom of religion is most precious and important. Benjamin Franklin once said, at a very critical time in history while the Constitution was being formed, "God governs in the affairs of men..." He was right. To try to govern one's life without God is like steering a ship without a compass or a rudder. One may drift along for a while, apparently successful, but sooner or later trouble will surface.

Politics affects our personal lives. German politics affected us in Holland in WWII big time. One difference between Hitler's Nazism and the United States is respect for God, which Hitler certainly did not have. As the Bible says, "When the righteous are in authority, the people rejoice, but when a wicked man rules, the people groan" (Proverbs 29:2). How true! The Bible also says, "Blessed is the nation whose God is the Lord, the people He has chosen as His own inheritance" (Psalm 33:12). "Righteousness (in right standing with God) exalts a nation, but sin is a reproach to any people" (Proverbs 14:24). These words speak volumes, as they apply to each country as well as to each individual, politically, spiritually, and physically.

In dealing with others, whether it is a person, a businessman, or a leader of a country, one can always ask the question, silently or vocally, "Are you a healer or a destroyer?" God heals and Satan destroys. "God is love," (1 John 4:8b). Love is so much better than destruction and killings.

One could conclude that today, if you...

- Are not registered to vote (because you don't want to be called for jury duty)
- Are registered to vote but don't bother to vote

- Are not interested in and keep up with the political developments in Washington, DC, as well as the happenings in your state capital, the county government, and the courts
- Never communicate with your local and federal representatives
- Do not pray for elected and appointed officials regularly ("Prayers…be made…for all who are in authority, that we may lead a quiet and peaceable life," 1 Tim.2:1-2) (I like that kind of life, and the fanatics don't)
- Do not pray for the country and our military regularly, (peace through strength)
- You think that these bad things just cannot and will not happen to America (Are we not vulnerable?)

…then you may be contributing to a possible demise of America. Of course, I hope this is not the case and that America will reign victorious in these challenging times.

So the crux of most of our problems today in America is that we have forgotten God, as Solzhenitsyn and Lincoln expressed in their days. There are still some Americans who remain very faithful to God. The God we have forgotten also loves Israel. God told Abraham, "I will make you a great nation; I will bless you and make your name great; and you shall be a blessing. I will bless those who bless you, and I will curse him who curses you, and in you all the families of the earth will be blessed" (Genesis 12:2-3 NKJV), which hopefully includes America, you, and me.

So, who wins? Tyrants seem to win occasionally, but their victories are short-lived, temporary really, with lots of damage and loss of many lives. God wins, with freedom, in the long run every time. Where is ultimate freedom? With God in heaven.

ENDNOTES

INVASION

1 Information taken from lecture delivered by Anthony Anderson at the University of Southern California, Oct. 17, 1995

INSIDE OUR APARTMENT

2 www.hacres.com referral #38451

FORTY YEARS OF DENTISTRY AND FAMILY LIFE

3 *Encyclopedia Britannica.* 1768, p.151-153, Book 7. Wm. Benton, Publ.

4 "7 Brothers For America." *The Index Journal of Greenwood, South Carolina.* July 21, 2005.

5 Genesis 1:1-3, 26, John 1:1, 2 and 14

6 Ephesians 3: 14–21

THE HUNT FOR JEWISH PEOPLE

7 "The Road to Neunburg", The Baltimore Sun - Todd Richissin, May 2, 2005.

Top from left to right: Jenn, Alan, Martin, Becky, Reese, Stephanie, Simon, John G, Rebecca, Marco

Lower: Alyssa, Blake, John, Tyler, Tori, Linda